Hunting
Big-Woods
Bucks

Secrets of Tracking
& Stalking Deer

Brian Stewart of Pennsylvania with a big woods buck he took while tracking with Hal Blood.

OUTDOORSMAN'S EDGE®

GUIDES

HUNTING BIG-WOODS BUCKS

SECRETS OF TRACKING & STALKING DEER

Hal Blood

CRE★TIVE OUTDOORS™

Trade paperback edition frist published in 2004 by

CRE A TIVE
OUTDOORS™

An imprint of Creative Homeowner®, Upper Saddle River, N.J.
Creative Homeowner® is a registered trademark of Federal Marketing Corporation.

Copyright © 2003 Woods N' Water, Inc. and Bookspan
All Rights Reserved

Brief quotations may be used in article reviews. For any other reproduction of the book including electronic, mechanical, photographic, recording, CD-ROM, videotaping, laser or computer disc, or other means, written permission must first be obtained from copyright holder and the publisher.

Front Cover Photo: Don Jones
Back Cover and Interior Photos (unless otherwise noted): Cedar Ridge Outfitters
Cover Design: Design Source Creative Services
Illustrations courtesy Katie Nesslerode

Printed in the United States of America
Current printing (last digit) 10 9 8 7 6 5 4
Library of Congress card number: 2004103775
ISBN: 1-58011-219-6

CREATIVE HOMEONWER®
24 Park Way
Upper Saddle River, NJ 07458

TABLE OF CONTENTS

ACKNOWLEDGEMENTS

I could never have written this book without the encouragement of many friends and fellow hunters.

Thanks to the clients who have become friends as we shared hunting camps—especially those who trusted me before I had proven myself. Without you, I could not have had the wonderful experiences I describe in this book in pursuit of big-woods bucks.

Thanks especially to Sue Morse for making me take the time to photograph the many forms of deer sign and for her willingness to let me include some of her personal photos in this book. Thanks to my niece Katie Nesselrode for drawing the illustrations.

Thanks to all of the guides who have worked for me over the years—your dedication and professionalism have helped to make my business as successful as it is.

Thanks to my wife, Deb, and my son, Gary, for putting up with a deer-hunting fanatic all these years and not complaining about my absence during deer season. I love you both dearly.

A special thanks to Peter and Kate Fiduccia for guiding me through this undertaking and organizing everything I have written.

Last, but not least, I thank the good Lord for all of His creations and the ability to enjoy them.

—Hal

INTRODUCTION

HUNTING BIG WOODS BUCKS is certain to become a classic among authoritative white-tailed deer hunting books, for it offers much for the seasoned and new hunter alike. As a "new hunter" who started deer and elk hunting in my early forties, I spent several years trying this and trying that. However, it was not until I booked a one-on-one hunt with Hal as my guide that I began the immensely rewarding journey of successful deer hunting. Mind you, I am a professional wildlife ecologist, forester, and tracker, so I was not exactly a novice in the woods. Now, eight years later, I've spent hundreds of hours with Hal scouting, stalking, and interpreting deer sign. Learning how to anticipate a big buck's whereabouts in a very big woods is just part of the incredible bounty of knowledge I've gained through my friendship with Hal.

In today's world, where so many young hunters may not have the benefit of learning the sport from parents and grandparents, and where more and more folks grow up in urban settings, the uncanny skills Hal shares in this book are all the more vital if hunting is to be a successful and fulfilling endeavor. In the big woods—where huge, mature, older-age-class bucks are more plentiful than in other eco-regions, yet where deer densities are decidedly lower—one must have a pretty good idea of where to look, when to stalk, and when to stand.

Hunting step-for-step with Hal over miles of terrain, I have marveled at his superb woodsmanship and tracking skills. Most of all, I have been repeatedly flabbergasted by Hal's in-depth knowledge of deer behavior coupled with his instincts for how to locate and get closer to wary bucks—no matter how wide-ranging their travels or big their terrain. Hal Blood's whitetail hunting techniques are the epitome of fair chase and consistent success, and I look forward to sharing the hunt with Hal and his wife Debbie every November! If you have longed for the skills to truly hunt big deer in the North Woods, you'll enjoy learning what Hal has to offer in this book.

Susan C. Morse
Ecologist
Founder, Keeping Track, Inc.

Good friend and guide Rick Jewell with his 242-pound six-pointer.

THE MAKING OF A GUIDE

I feel fortunate that I grew up in a hunting family. I can remember as a little boy waiting eagerly for my father to come home from hunting. Sometimes he had rabbits, sometimes pheasants—and sometimes nothing. I was the most eager for his arrival home during deer season, on the chance that he had been lucky enough to get a deer. I grew up in rural southern Maine, and at that time there were not a lot of deer in the area. Dad always worked two jobs, so his hunting time was limited, and with five kids to feed he was never fussy about whether he shot a buck or a doe.

When he did manage to get a deer, I went to the garage every day to admire the beauty and sleekness of the creature, and I always asked when I could go deer hunting. When I was about six years old he finally broke down and took me with him, knowing that his chances for success were slim with me tagging along. I've often wondered how many fathers would be willing to sacrifice their hunt to get a new hunter started.

On those first outings I carried a toy version of a Model 94 Winchester. From my plastic rifle I moved up to a Daisy BB gun—the model 94 version. When I turned ten, I finally started carrying a real gun—a Model 94 Winchester 30-30. It was special, as it was the one my grandfather had given to my father. I loved that gun and cleaned and oiled it every time I used it. I have since passed it on to my son, and I hope the tradition continues.

MY FIRST DEER

I shot my first deer when I was twelve—a nice fat spike horn. Dad had taken me in on a ridge near our camp. I sat looking one way while he watched the other way about thirty feet from me. We hadn't been there five minutes when I saw a deer running toward me. I pulled the gun up, took the safety off, and the buck stopped about thirty yards from me. POW! He dropped in his tracks. Dad ran over—said he thought I'd shot myself! I said, Nope, I got him. I think Dad was more excited than I was, especially when he found out I'd forgotten my hunting license! He was looking over his shoulder as he gutted the buck. We covered him with leaves and hurried back to camp to call Mom and have her bring my license. I shot a doe the next year in a spot I found on my own. By then I had the whitetail bug, and it will never go away.

1

Dad used to hunt at the "lodge," a place in mid-coast Maine that his cousins and a friend owned. I had heard stories of all the deer there and really wanted to go with him, but Dad didn't want me to miss school. Finally, when I was sixteen and had begged for two years, he let me miss a week of school to go. Dad couldn't take time off work, so his cousin Stan took me under his wing. There were about eight regulars at the lodge, and we had a whole mountain to ourselves.

The method they used was to sit in the morning and evening and still-hunt during

Left to right: Dad, my brother Todd, and me in the early days up north.

the day. I'd sit a little in the morning, but then I always had to see what was over the next ridge. (In my earlier hunts with my dad, we did a lot of sitting, which probably explains why today I can sit only long enough to eat a sandwich.) And I didn't ride back to the lodge for breakfast with the others; I preferred to hunt my way back and find where the deer were so I'd be able to help plan the day's hunt. When I got back to camp, the older guys asked where the deer were and how they could get one. Always knowing where there were some deer became my mission. I managed to shoot a deer every year I was there, and it's where I shot my first big buck, a 208-pound seven-pointer.

When I was eighteen I enlisted in the Marine Corps. I even planned my graduation date from boot camp so I had my ten days leave during deer season. The whole time I was in the marines, I managed to get home every year for deer season and always got my deer. I had every intention of becoming a game warden when I got out of the service, but my hopes were dashed when Maine's Fish and Wildlife Department was not accepting applications the year I was discharged.

I got married during my last year in the marines, to a special girl I had met just before going to boot camp. Our only prenuptial agreement was that Deb would never interfere with my hunting and fishing. I can honestly say that this agreement has worked, as we are in our twenty-sixth year of marriage and she's not only kept the agreement, but she's also joined me in my pursuits and has taken a couple of big bucks herself. Since becoming a game warden wasn't possible when I was discharged, I took a job in a grocery warehouse. It was inside work and I hated it, but I did get a week of vacation during deer season. I had to take a week when the season was open only up north, and that's when my big-woods buck training years started.

When I was a teenager, I starting going fishing in the Jackman area with the boys from the lodge. We always saw lots of deer and deer tracks on these trips, so it seemed like a logical place to hunt during my week of vacation. I had to talk someone else into going with me, and Dad volunteered to be the first guinea pig, so we borrowed his cousin Stan's pop-up camper and headed north. It was the first week of November, and we weren't prepared for the weather. It went down to the single digits at night and got up to maybe freezing during the day. We had a Coleman stove, a lantern, and a heater. When we cooked in the evening, it got warm and steamy, and the condensation froze on the roof panels. In the morning, when we lit the stove, it would be like a rainstorm inside as the ice on the panels melted. We had no way to dry our clothes or boots, so when we put them on in the morning we had to run around to get everything thawed out.

Needless to say, it was quite an experience, and one that Dad wouldn't repeat until we had a better place to stay. We had snow only one day, and I was able to follow the track of a big buck, but I never saw him—only heard him running ahead of me. I did shoot a spikehorn the last day of our hunt. He had one spike and white ears and legs.

A successful week's hunt in a remote big woods deer camp.

After I got back, I quit my job in the warehouse and went into lobstering with my father-in-law. Now I wasn't limited to the first week of the season. I recruited a bigger group for the next trip—my wife Deb and my brother Todd joined Dad and me. Cousin Stan let us borrow a bigger camper he had recently purchased, and we were a lot more comfortable. We didn't get snow that year either, but we did get two deer. My brother shot a doe and I shot a seven-point buck.

The next year I bought a fixer-upper thirty-two-foot mobile home. I towed it up north, and now we had a base camp. Over the next few years various friends hunted with us. I started going later in the season so I'd have snow to track on, and track I did. I chased bucks through swamps, over mountains, and everywhere in between. I spent so much time chasing them that all I ever saw was the back end of a running buck! I think I chased every buck in the township at least twice. I never was a patient person (just ask my wife), but I knew that if I was ever going to get a big-woods buck, I'd have to learn to have some patience.

After two years lobstering with my father-in-law, I started my own lobstering business. Now that I had a business to pay for as well as a household to support, I had to put my nose to the grindstone and didn't get to hunt as much as I wanted to. I took only a few days here and there when the weather was too bad to haul lobster traps. To make matters worse, the deer herd was declining in the area we'd been hunting. There were some bad winters in the mid-eighties with a lot of logging going on around in the deeryards, and an increasing coyote population took its toll on the deer in some northern areas. I realized that I'd have to learn to hunt smarter to make my limited time count. I left the camper in town for the next couple of years and studied the topo maps for new areas to check out. I was also considering the possibility of buying a sporting camp, as I was beginning to realize that lobstering was not the best occupation for a person who loves to hunt and fish.

Since I wouldn't get much time to hunt during the next two years, I knew I'd

A large boat can take enough equipment to spend the week in the woods. Usually by late season most lakes are frozen, so plan an early season trip.

have to slow down and be patient when I *did* get a chance to hunt instead of trying to run the deer into the next county. Both of those years I shot a ten-pointer on my first day of hunting. One was 185 pounds and the other was 213 pounds. I shot them while I was tracking, about a quarter mile apart on the same ridge.

What a feeling of accomplishment that was for me—

I had figured out some keys to successful buck hunting! By then I knew that hunting a few days a season or even a few days a week would never satisfy me. I knew that having a sporting camp and guiding was what I wanted to do with my life. I took the all the tests and got my Master's Guide License. Deb and I decided to find a piece of property and build our own sporting camp. In the spring of 1988, I found my property. I say *my* property, since Deb was not thrilled with the junk vehicles on the land. I urged her to have a vision of what could be, and she bought into that vision. We made plans to build our first cabin the following spring. With the help of my carpenter buddy Ricky, we cleaned out the lot and built a cabin, and the next year I guided my very first clients, Mark and Chris, from Rhode Island. One year later we sold the lobstering business, built another cabin, and moved north. The next year we built another cabin and the house I had promised Deb for her support of my dream.

My first big woods deer camp.

Meanwhile, I started guiding remote tent-camp hunts, always trying to get as far as possible from other hunters. (I've always had a psychological quirk—if I see another hunter in the woods, I think that all the deer have been run off.) I've had a lot of fun over the years on these tent-camp hunts. Some have been more successful than others, but we've always managed to have good people in camp who tell stories of their encounters with big-woods bucks.

Since I've been guiding, I don't get to hunt by myself as much as I used to. The trade-off is that I get to spend the whole season in pursuit of big-woods bucks while helping other hunters to realize their dreams—hunters who are out making a living in this hectic world and don't have time to gain the experience to be as successful a hunter as I am. And although I haven't had much time to hunt myself, I *have* managed to take thirteen big-woods bucks in the last fifteen years, and eight of them dressed out at over two hundred pounds. I've also been able to experience more of nature's wonderful offerings than most people experience in a lifetime. And at forty-six years of age, as I sit and reflect on all of this, I realize I'm just getting started. ■

Mike Penn from New Jersey with his first big woods buck: seven points, 205 pounds.

THE NOMADIC WHITETAIL

The big-woods bucks is a nomad. He has no established boundaries. He is free to roam wherever he chooses in the wide expanse of the North. Unlike his suburban and rural cousins to the south who contend with paved roads, houses, fences, and other unnatural barriers, there are no limits on the nomad. He doesn't rely on the farmer to plant food; he travels throughout his territory feeding and bedding where he chooses. His cousins are used to the sounds of car horns, tractors, and people's voices. That's why they establish safe bedding areas and trails that lead to and from them. Their life revolves around human activity.

The nomad is in tune with his natural surroundings and flees at the slightest noise or movement he doesn't recognize—he'll run to the nearest cover and wait to see if he's being pursued. He's learned over thousands of years of being chased by wolves, bears, and cats not to waste his energy or run blindly into another predator. In all my years of hunting, I've never had a big buck that I've spooked stop in the open and present me with a shot. I *have* seen many smaller bucks stop, which is the reason they get culled from the gene pool. The nomad will stop behind trees or brush, where all you might see is the flick of his tail or the glint of his antlers.

The nomad knows where all the does in his territory are, and as the rut approaches, he begins to check each one to see if she's ready for him. He knows each doe by smell like high school boys know the names of all the girls in their classes. When he's satisfied that every doe in his territory has been bred, he'll travel to other territories to seek out does that may have been overlooked.

Winters in the North can be brutal, and the ground can be snow-covered from November through April. Where feed is marginal in deer wintering areas (deeryards), Mother Nature will control the population, assuring that the strongest survive to reproduce.

NOMAD SIZE

The nomad is the largest of his species. The heaviest buck taken in Maine—by Horace Hinkley in 1955 near Bingham—field dressed at three hundred and fifty-five pounds. He would have been well over four hundred pounds live weight. Almost every year a buck is taken in Maine that weighs around three hundred

These hunters may have been the first people these bucks encountered.

pounds field-dressed. In the big woods of the North it is common for one out of every six bucks tagged to field dress at 200 pounds or more. Two hundred is the magic number that qualifies an animal for entry into the Biggest Bucks in Maine.

DEER POPULATIONS

Deer densities are relatively low in the North. I've found areas where the population is as low as five deer per square mile. I've also found areas that may have as many as twenty-five deer per square mile, but there's no way to tell for certain. I believe these differences are due to the types of cover and the quality of wintering habitat in different areas. It doesn't seem to matter how many other deer live in an area, a nomad will always be there, too.

The nomad is a rule-breaker by nature. He doesn't always behave in a way that is considered "normal." That's why we have to hunt him on his own terms while we're on his turf. Don't necessarily expect him to winter in a deeryard. He's often content to stay by himself on a remote mountaintop. On many occasions when snowshoeing in the winter, I've discovered lone bucks in their hideouts. I find that

He's growing a trophy rack, feeding around this mineral-rich swale bog.

they use the same bed all winter, and it may be as big as a bathtub. They make trails ranging out a hundred yards or so in every direction for feeding ventures. I think they feel secure in these places, knowing that the coyotes will follow the other deer—the majority—to their established yards.

FOLLOWING A NOMAD THROUGH THE SEASONS

Let's look at how a nomad leads his life by following him through the four seasons and seeing what he might encounter.

SPRING: Spring is the time of renewal. The melting snows wash away signs of winter. Green plants start to spring up, giving deer and other animals much-needed nutrition. If the deer are lucky, this takes place by early April. If they are not, it might not happen until early May. In late-spring years an old nomad may perish if the previous fall's rut left him in poor condition. If he survived the winter, he comes down

This buck is new to the world. If you look closely you can see the pedicles that someday will grow a heavy set of antlers. (Courtesy: Susan C. Morse)

from his winter hideout to a south-facing hardwood ridge or a chopping (a place where loggers have cut trees) where the sun has melted the snow and new sprouts are poking up. If he traveled to a deeryard the previous fall, he may have traveled as many as thirty miles to get there. Now he makes his way back to his familiar haunts.

He doesn't move much this time of year, but eats constantly to replace the weight he lost over the winter. If he had a good winter and is in relatively good shape, his antlers begin to grow in late April. At this time he also loses his gray winter coat and replaces it with a rusty red summer one. By late May, there is rich vegetation everywhere. He spends most of his days just feeding and trying to keep swarms of bugs away. He may join up with some other bucks—they're not a threat to him at this time of year and he tolerates their company.

SUMMER: By July his antlers have grown to their full shape and number of points. He's back in good physical shape and may wander about his territory finding the best places to feed. He beds down where he feeds since the summer foliage gives him plenty of cover. He continues this pattern through August, but when September arrives, there's a transformation.

FALL: Decreasing daylight triggers his antlers to stop growing and the velvet covering to split and peel off. He leaves his bachelor friends, preferring solitude as

This young buck is already displaying the alertness he will need to grow to a ripe old age. (Courtesy: Susan C. Morse)

he polishes his antlers and strengthens his neck for the battles to come. By October he has replaced his summer coat with the darker brown/gray one that will gradually thicken to take him through the winter. By mid-October, the fall colors have come and gone and the leaves on the ground cover all signs of his summer hideouts.

This is the time when he makes a transition to his fall hideouts, since the fallen leaves have opened up the woods and made him easier to see. He returns to the ridges and swamps that have provided him security in the past. He's in the best shape of his life and is saving his energy, because the time is fast approaching when he'll travel day and night to seek out does to carry on his legacy.

By early November he starts to travel his territory, checking his signposts to see if there is a challenger to his superiority. His neck swells and strengthens as he spars with trees to prepare himself in case he meets a challenger he cannot bluff. By mid-November he's found a doe ready to breed. He stays with her for a couple of days to make sure his job is done. After that he's off to look for the next doe, and

This buck is losing the velvet from his antlers. He will soon start to spar with trees to strenghten his neck for battles he may have to fight with other bucks. (Courtesy: Susan C. Morse)

the process continues until he's sure all the does in his territory are bred.

Now there's snow on the ground, and one day while lying on one of his favorite bluffs he spots something familiar following his track. He's been followed by hunters before and instinctively knows what to do. He slips from his bed and runs down the back side of the bluff and up on the next

Bucks spend most of their time during the summer months feeding and laying around. (Courtesy: Susan C. Morse)

bluff and stands waiting to see if the hunters will follow. He plays hide and seek like this all day, but the hunters are nothing more than an irritation, and by nightfall they're gone—he's won the game again.

WINTER: By early December he's lost a lot of weight, but not the desire to spread his genes. He feeds and rests more, but still makes excursions to unfamiliar territory on the chance he might find a receptive doe. This is the time when some healthy doe fawns may be able to breed, and he is fully aware of it.

The December snows pile up, and most of the other deer go to wintering areas, but the nomad decides to stay on his favorite mountain. He knows this place has a good canopy of spruce trees and enough browse—moss and twigs—to carry him

This buck is enjoying the sun on a cold winter day. He will be dropping his antlers any day now.

through the long winter ahead. Through January and February he gets out of his bed only to feed. He knows it's critical to conserve energy by staying curled up. The temperature drops to thirty degrees below zero on some nights and the winds howl, but he knows he can survive as he has many winters before.

In March there's a thaw and a freeze, and the crust on the snow holds his weight. He can now venture out farther for a fresh supply of browse. He won't go too far though, since he knows that if there's another thaw, he could sink through the snow and be stranded.

April comes again and another year has passed in the life of the nomad. He overcame his struggles, and now he's free to wander again with no boundaries.

Somehow I don't think the nomad would want it any other way. ∎

A good week's hunt in the north woods at Cedar Ridge Lodge. The bucks on the left are 125- and 155-pound yearlings. The bucks on the right weigh 263 and 260 pounds. All these bucks carry the genetics for large bodies.

Chris DiPalmer with his Thanksgiving-week buck, a nice eight-pointer that weighed 230 pounds.

TALKING TO DEER

Volumes have been written over the past fifteen years about calling deer, and most hunters have seen at least one video or television show on calling techniques, what brand of call is best, and when to use a specific call. I know this, as I've watched them, too. All of these shows have a guy or gal sitting in a tree stand or a ground blind, and all of them are about hunting around farm country or food plots where deer are concentrated. There's nothing wrong with these techniques, but they won't help you much if you're headed to the north country in search of a big-woods buck.

In the big woods you can blow a call or rattle horns until the cows come home—but if a buck can't hear you, he won't come. I'm not saying calling doesn't work, because it works fine, but you have to learn when and where to call to make it effective. Some days I never take a call out and other days I use one quite often, but I always carry a grunt tube and a snort call. Often they've made the difference in shooting a buck or not.

RATTLING

Rattling is the type of calling I use least—not because it's ineffective, but because I'm usually still-hunting or tracking, and I just don't like to carry the antlers around. I did try a rattling bag, but I still consider it excess baggage. If I *do* rattle, it's during the first week of the season when there may not be snow on the ground. I'll still-hunt around and try rattling when I think I'm near a buck's bedding area.

> ### TRYING OUT A RATTLING BAG
>
> One time I was still-hunting along the base of a ridge. I knew there was a brook off to my left on the other side of some thick spruce knolls—just the kind of place where bucks like to hang out. I came to a place where a spring seeping down a ravine had formed a slough hole—one of those places where black mud goes over your boots and if you don't get out quickly enough your boots fill with water. I saw quite a few rubs on the brown ash trees scattered around the area. It was time to stop for my ten o'clock sandwich, so I figured I might as well try rattling. I'd just bought a rattling bag and was eager to see if it would work.

I took the rattling bag and my sandwich out of my belt pack and gave the bag a good shake. I was leaning up against a big cedar tree enjoying my sandwich (I can't stand being stuck out in the open) when I heard sticks breaking on the spruce knoll in front of me. I had just stuck my sandwich in my pocket when I saw a brown body come through the small firs and out of the green growth. I got ready for the big rack I knew must be ahead of that body. All the time I was thinking, *This rattling thing really works!* Just then he busted out of the thicket and stopped. A nice fat crotch-horn! He looked around and then proceeded up the ravine. When he got out about fifty yards I gave him a grunt and he turned around and looked back. I watched him poke around for a while; then he went on his way and I went on mine.

Since then I've rattled that bag many times and have never brought another buck in. I think I was lucky: I happened to be close enough for him to hear me, *and* I called from a spot used by bucks. 〓

Sometimes I do use a set of rattling antlers. During opening week every year I guide the same hunter—Sue Morse from Vermont—and she is fit enough to go anywhere I want to go. We always like to explore new areas and see what we might find. If there's no tracking snow I'll take antlers in my day pack. If the leaves are cold and crunchy in the morning, we'll hike in to a spot and try rattling until it warms up and the frost is out of the leaves.

ONE SUCCESS WITH RATTLING ANTLERS

One morning we walked in about a mile on an old winter road. A winter road is a logging road used only in the winter, so the brush grows back after a few years. I had picked out a spot while scouting that overlooked some old choppings and beaver bogs. It was a cold, clear morning—the kind when sound travels a long distance. We got settled into our spot just as dawn approached. I set off a good fight with the antlers that lasted about a minute, then set them down and waited. I tried this about every ten minutes. After about half an hour, I heard crunching on the road off to my right. I leaned forward to look around the corner, and there was another hunter sneaking down the road! My heart sank. He waved and turned around. I was very surprised that there was anyone else way back here. My plan for the morning was to still-hunt even deeper, so I told Sue we'd go now before we got interrupted again. We put on our packs and started easing down the road. We had gone only about a hundred yards when off to our left in the thick brush a buck snorted, took a couple of jumps, and stopped. His snort was one of those deep ones that you can tell comes out of a big chest. I tried grunting, but he paid no attention and snuck away. I'm sure he had spotted us coming down the road. He had to have been coming toward my rattling—if we had stayed put, he would have stepped out within seventy-five yards of us.

Of all the many times I've tried the rattling horns, that's the only time I remember when I had a response. Other hunters I know, as well as some of the guides who work for me, have rattled in bucks big and small, so I know rattling works on big-woods bucks. The key is to pick the right spot and be persistent.

SNORTING

Not many people try to call deer by snorting or "blowing." In fact, you might wonder why someone would use a call that alerts deer or represents danger. I used to think that way too, until I started experimenting with snorting. I noticed that besides snorting as an alert, deer also snort to locate each other and will sometimes snort simply to clear their nostrils so they can scent better.

A bleat call may bring in a doe. During the rut you'll want to keep an eye out for a buck that may follow. (Courtesy: Susan C. Morse)

A long time ago, I bought an Alaskan rubber-band call. When you blow softly on it, it imitates a doe bleat. I tried it quite a bit without any luck. I figured that the sound was so low a deer would almost have to be in view to hear it. One day I blew on it hard to clear out some duff. Lo and behold, it sounded just like a deer snorting, and it was loud enough to carry quite a distance!

From then on, whenever I spook a deer, I pull out the old Alaskan call and blow a few times. Sometimes they stop in their tracks, and sometimes they run just out of sight, but they stop almost every time I blow, and often they snort back. The big bucks always make sure they're out of sight before they stop.

USING MY TRUSTY ALASKAN CALL

One time in a remote camp all the guys were posted in stands or still-hunting. I was scouting an area that had a bunch of spruce knolls and ravines. I was coming down from a knoll through some short firs, and a spikehorn jumped up in front of me and bounded down the hill. I grabbed my Alaskan call and gave it a good blow, and that spike stopped dead in his tracks. I was just watching him look back when I

Mark's seven pointer that came sneaking back through the fog after I snorted. We spooked the buck and two does as we still-hunted a hardwood ridge.

heard *boom!* He jumped into the air, did a thirty-yard dash, and piled up on the ground. Little did I know that one of my hunters had been picking his way through the woods and had just stopped to look around when I spooked that buck. Talk about two points connecting. Lucky day for Bobby, but not for the spike.

Another time I had taken a hunter, Mark, with me. We had picked up a nice buck track and were headed up the mountain. It had warmed up and rained during the night, so very little snow was left. By the time we reached a chopping high on the mountain, the snow was washed away. From what little of the tracks we could see, it looked as though the buck had gone higher up the mountain and then had run back down. I thought our best bet was to still-hunt our way across the mountain at the edge of the green growth. I put Mark about thirty yards to my right and we started across. I don't think we went more than a hundred yards over a little rise when I saw three tails waving away through the fog. I was reaching for my call when I noticed that there was a rack above the last one. I whispered *buck* to Mark just as they disappeared into the mist. I gave a few blows, waited a minute, and gave a few more. It was very quiet that day, and I started to hear footsteps coming towards us. I saw Mark raise his gun, and the shooting started. I don't know how many shots he fired, but when everything was quiet we walked over and found that he had himself a nice seven-pointer.

I think that buck thought my snorting was either another buck he would challenge to keep the does he had with him or another doe he could check out. From my experience listening to deer snort over the years, one thing I'm sure of is that if you hear a single deep, long snort, it's usually a good buck. If you hear multiple short, quick blasts, more than likely it's a doe or a yearling buck.

GRUNTING

The grunt call is probably the most widely used deer call. Nowadays you see very few hunters who don't have one hanging around their neck. Grunt calls work great in the big woods as long as you keep in mind that *you have to be close enough to a buck for him to hear it.* I've seen hunters walking around aimlessly through the woods blowing on their grunt tubes. If you do that, there's no way you can pay attention to what's going on around you. The grunt is my favorite call, but I rarely use it unless I'm reasonably sure a buck is around. Usually this means I've either seen or heard a deer.

GRUNTING ATTRACTS BIG BUCKS

One morning I was headed up a mountain in a few inches of fresh snow. It was one of those gray days with snow spitting from the clouds—the kind of day you dream about, with the snow so quiet you can hear the flakes hitting your hat. I came across some tracks where does had fed during the night. A little higher up, I cut an average-size buck track with just a dusting of snow in it. I decided to follow it and see where it might lead me. The trail meandered across the ridge and then headed up higher. I followed it up a steep softwood knoll with blowdowns scattered about. It went under a blowdown so close to the ground that I had to get on my hands and knees to get under it. Just as I stood up, I saw a flash of brown disappear into the first thirty feet to my left. I snatched the grunt tube out of my jacket and blew two quick grunts. I stood silent and waited. In a few minutes the firs started to move, and out stepped the buck. He was a nice and sleek, and I guessed he'd dress out at 180 pounds. He had long, curved beams that forked at the end, but no other points—not a buck I was interested in shooting. I still had the grunt tube to my lips, so I grunted again to see what his response would be. Each time I grunted, he looked my way and then looked around. After about five minutes he'd had enough and bounded up the mountain.

Another time I had just posted one of my hunters on stand. I came back out to the road and decided to look around for a track. There was about six inches of snow with a good crust on top. Not the best tracking conditions, but I figured if I could get a buck moving he might travel down the rub line my hunter was posted on. I didn't get far down the road when I cut a nice buck track that hadn't even set up yet—the snow where he had broken the crust was still soft. I knew he couldn't be far, since deer don't like to travel much when there's a hard crust on the snow. I started following him, placing my toes in his tracks, trying not to make much noise. After only a couple of hundred yards up over a hardwood knoll, I heard him break the crust in a slashy chopping (an area so thick with new tree growth that one can barely see twenty yards) to my right. The brush was so thick it looked like a wall. I sat down, got out my grunt tube, and gave a few grunts. I heard the crunch of another deer above me. I grunted off and on for about ten minutes, but the woods remained silent. I knew the deer were still standing there, as there was no way for them to sneak away in the crust without my hearing them.

I decided to stop grunting and just wait. In about five minutes the

The buck I call Thin Horns. I shot this long bodied 235-pound eight-pointer after stopping him with a grunt call. It took two days to get him off the mountain.

crust started breaking again off to my right, and the sound was getting closer. The buck was coming straight at me. The brush started parting around his horns and he stepped out about twenty yards away on the other side of a blowdown. He walked around the blowdown and stopped fifteen feet away staring right at me. What a sight! He had a beautiful wide, heavy rack with only six points. He had one of those Holstein necks and would weigh well over two hundred pounds dressed. I put my head down and looked out from under my hat brim to avoid making eye contact. Not finding another buck around, he walked out through the hardwoods in search of a doe. It was his lucky day, as I had tagged out the week before.

When I'm tracking in quiet conditions on a very still day and I spook a buck, I'll sometimes grunt a couple of times as the he runs. Because it's quiet, he can hear the grunts and may stop, thinking I'm another buck. One time this paid off for me with a 235-pound eight-pointer. I had picked up his track where he had been checking some does. He left the does and headed into some fir thickets near the top of the mountain. As I followed his track through a thicket he almost had to tunnel through, I heard a swish to my left and caught a flash of brown twenty feet away. I grabbed my grunt tube and gave three grunts before easing my way out of the firs to a place where I'd be able to see. As I moved ahead I saw a ravine in front of me, and I slowly eased ahead so I could look across it. Just then I saw the buck bolt from behind a blowdown and run down the ravine. It was a bad choice of directions for that buck, as my bullet found its mark on his second jump. He had stopped in the ravine after hearing my grunt, giving me a chance I would not otherwise have had.

All of these times I knew a buck was around and used the grunt to turn the odds in my favor, but I've done the same thing in other circumstances with no results. It just goes to show you that you can fool some of the bucks some of the time, but you can't fool all the bucks all of the time!

In my experience, most of the time grunting in the big woods attracts either dominant bucks or yearling bucks. My theory is that the dominant bucks are usually up for a challenge, and the yearling bucks don't know any better—they haven't been challenged by a dominant buck as they are not considered a threat. Subordinate bucks, on the other hand, don't answer grunts because they've experienced being challenged by a dominant buck and don't want to experience it again.

TWO THAT GOT AWAY

One morning Sue and I were sneaking along a skid trail (where loggers skid logs out) beside a stream. It was fairly thick with firs and brush around a beaver bog. I heard a crack and looked up to see a deer jump across the trail fifty yards ahead. Not being able to see horns, but knowing the deer was alone, I thought there was a good chance it was a buck. I started grunting and we moved up and found a comfortable spot on a log to sit. In front of us the trail split and we could see down both branches. After about ten minutes, I saw a small buck sneak across the left fork and go into the thick firs. We could hear him moving around but couldn't see into the thicket. I teased him with a series of grunts, hoping to coax him into the open. A few minutes later I caught a movement to our right. A big buck stepped across the right fork of the trail, stopped between the two forks, and stared toward us. He was an eight- or ten-pointer and was only about forty yards away in the brush. We quickly forgot about the other buck and focused on this one. I was sure Sue would get him, as he had to cross one of the trails to go anywhere. Just as I was trying to get her focused on the buck, he slipped back across the same trail and disappeared. I waited a few minutes and grunted again, and it wasn't long before he appeared in the brush again to our right. Again, just before Sue could get lined up he turned and disappeared into the brush like a ghost.

We couldn't believe we had called in two bucks at the same time and let them both get away! I think the small buck had come back out of curiosity. The big buck could smell him, thought the smaller one might be getting some doe action, and had to check it out. Not smelling any does in the area, he decided to leave.

The nice thing about a grunt call is that it's easy to carry and you can use it whether you're stand-hunting, still-hunting, or tracking. The snort call is also easy to carry, and it's best suited for tracking or still-hunting. Rattling horns are are best suited for stand-hunting—they're bulky to carry while still-hunting or tracking. When you're stand-hunting, I suggest rattling at fifteen- to twenty-minute intervals with the idea of drawing bucks that might be traveling through the area beyond your sight.

Whatever call you decide to use, remember that calling implies to deer that you are one of them. It's important to try to sound as realistic as possible. If you're not able to spend enough time in the woods to listen to live deer, at least watch some videos or television shows about calling. That way, when the opportunity to talk to a deer arises, you'll have a better chance of sounding like one. ∎

Joe Smith and Bob Haggan from New Jersey with a pair of 225-pound, eight-pointers taken on their own while hunting from Cedar Ridge's lodge.

Mike Featherstone shot this 234-pound eight-point buck by understanding how to effectively hunt a primary scrape.

UNDERSTANDING RUBS AND SCRAPES

To understand the significance of rubs and the role they play to a big-woods buck, you have to accept the fact that you will not find as many of them in big-woods buck country as you might in other areas. A rub is a bare spot on a tree where a buck has removed the bark with his antlers. He does this to strengthen his neck muscles for the battling he may do over a doe. While making a rub, a buck also leaves scent from glands on his forehead as a calling card for other deer in the area. It's important to know what types of trees are most often rubbed so you don't spend a lot of time looking where there may not be any. It's also important to know *when* trees are being rubbed so you can plan successful scouting trips. And finally, it's important to know that every bare spot you find on a tree is not necessarily a buck rub. I've known hunters who identified what they thought were big-buck rubs that were actually moose rubs or places where moose had stripped bark from trees to eat.

In the late fall, after the moose rut is over and they're done thrashing around

This is the most impressive signpost rub I've ever found. This brown ash has been rubbed by several generations of bucks since it was small. There are tine marks in the bark five feet off the ground.

the alder patches, moose start rubbing the base of their antlers the same way a buck does. They usually do this on fir trees, which bucks don't often choose. Moose rubs are generally three to six feet above the ground, with whitetail buck rubs usually being about two to three feet above the ground. Moose also start stripping the bark from all types of maple trees—trees whose bark is still tender, which usually means those that are two to six inches in diameter. This is called *barking*. I don't know why they eat bark, but Sue Morse, a biologist I guide each year, theorizes that the bark contains a mineral they need. It's easy to distinguish barking from rubbing because you can see teeth marks in a tree that's been barked.

You might be thinking now that a course in *dendrology* (the study of trees) might be in order, and it's true that knowing trees will greatly help you in sorting things out when you hunt the big woods. Here's a list—in order of preference—of trees that bucks rub in the big woods (according to my observations): brown ash, beech, yellow birch, willow brush, spruce, alder, fir and striped maple. The first three probably account for seventy-five percent of all the rubs I find, and trees I didn't mention probably account for only one percent of the deer rubs I've observed.

Striped maples are last on the list and are least important. Bucks usually rub them as soon as the velvet on their antlers starts falling off, but I've seldom observed rubs on them after that. If you're scouting in late September or early October, you'll probably see rubs on striped maples, and this is a sign that bucks are in the area. Sometimes you'll find several of these rubs in one area, which usually indicates that a buck is spending quite a bit of time there.

SIGNPOST RUBS

When scouting for rubs, I follow a stream and then check all the springs that flow into it.

Number one on the list is the brown ash, the most important tree to a big-woods buck. Ninety-five percent of all the *signpost rubs* I've observed are made on this tree, so it's a good one to learn to identify. (What I call a "signpost" rub is one made more than two years in a row on the same tree.) Brown ash is not a prolific tree, and it grows fairly slowly. Its only commercial use is for making pack baskets, so it's not cut down often when an area is logged. It grows in wet areas, usually along streams and around spring seeps on hardwood ridges. I suspect it has a certain odor that attracts bucks.

The more years a signpost tree has been rubbed, the better an indication of

A buck rubbed this brown ash that had been scarred by a skidder tire (on the left side). A scar on a tree may be a visual cue for bucks to rub in the area or on the same tree.

This could be the start of a signpost. A big brown ash rubbed by a big buck for the first time.

buck activity it is, and I've found some that I believe have been rubbed for at least fifty years, with the peak of the rubbing occurring in the late fall. That's a lot of generations of bucks, and when you find one of these trees, you've found a gold mine, and it's even better if there are several in the same area. Bucks make signposts where their territories overlap. Like cities on a map with roads connecting them to other cities, signposts are at the convergence of several deer trails leading to other signposts. You can also consider a signpost as the hub of a spoked wheel. Bucks use these signposts to connect the dots throughout their territories. A buck uses a signpost tree more as a place to leave his scent than as a place to spar and strengthen his neck muscles. It's a place to leave his calling card—the scent from his forehead glands—for all of the other bucks to smell.

HUNTING A HUB

One season, in the first week of a remote hunt, my guides and I took the hunters to a new area we had scouted before the season started. We didn't get there until the middle of the week because a bad snowstorm kept us hunting closer to camp. Most of the guys posted up in the ground blinds we had built. I picked up a good track and was following it around the edge of a huge cedar swamp. The track dropped into a wet ravine where a spring was bubbling from the ground right into one of the best hubs I've ever found. Four major trails converged there, and I counted at least thirty brown ash rubs as I stood in one spot. As I continued following the buck, he turned onto another trail at the intersection and then went about fifty yards and started working a scrape.

I knew I had found a gold mine and had to get a hunter in here to take a stand. I built a makeshift blind on a boulder within sight of the hub and the scrape and had a hunter sit there for the last two days of that week. He sat in the morning and afternoon but came out for lunch. It was quite a walk to get back in to the blind, so he was killing about three

Mike's massive twelve pointer that grosses 184 B&C. Mike took the 245-pound buck while hunting out of a ground blind I built in a secluded cedar bog.

hours a day going back and forth. He never saw a buck, but I still felt we could be successful in that spot.

When the next group of hunters arrived in camp on Sunday, I asked for a volunteer who would commit to sitting at that stand all day for the entire week. A young fellow named Mike from Pennsylvania agreed to take the stand. We headed into the swamp early the next morning. I took Mike in while Fred, my other guide, posted up the others. It was a damp, balmy day, and most of the snow had melted off. I got Mike settled in the blind and took off to do more scouting. At eleven o'clock a shot echoed out of the swamp. I wasn't sure which hunter it was, so I waited for the signal shots we had told the hunters to fire if they were successful. There were no signal shots, so I continued my circle. At one o'clock two more shots rang out. I waited, and still no signal. I was a little frustrated, thinking that these hunters couldn't hit anything. Fifteen minutes later I heard another shot. By now I had worked my way closer to the hunters and knew it had to be Mike shooting. Five minutes later came the two signal shots. I rushed to Mike's spot in anticipation of seeing the buck he must have shot. As I was nearing him, I saw that Freddie had already arrived. He hollered to me that I'd better hold on to my hat, and he was right. It was a huge buck—at first all I could see were horns that looked like a hay rake. After the congratulations, we held a photo session as Mike told us his story.

After I'd dropped him off in the morning, Mike hung some doe-in-heat scent wafers in the trail twenty yards in front of him. At eleven o'clock he noticed a set of antlers coming up the trail toward him off to his right. At first glance he thought it was a moose, but as the body came into view he knew it was a big whitetail. The buck stopped to smell the scent wafers as Mike was putting the cross hairs on him. He fired and the buck reared up, fell over backwards, and lay there dead. He never fired signal shots, he said, because he didn't want to bother us. He thought he could drag the buck out by himself, but once he had it field-dressed and his rope tied to the horns, he knew he was going to need some help. It took Freddie and me all afternoon to drag that buck out of the swamp. When we got him on the camp scale that night, he pulled the pin down to 245 pounds. Not bad for a first Maine buck. ✺

Signpost rubs are the most important pieces of buck sign to a hunter in the big woods. Signposts can narrow your search for places bucks hide and travel. The area around signpost rubs is a good place to take a stand, to still-hunt, and to pick up a track when there's snow. The more signposts there are in an area, the better your chances of connecting with a buck.

SCRAPES

Scrapes are another type of buck sign that has been written and talked about in hunting circles for years. We've all heard the scientific research results about why, when, and where they are made. I've come to the conclusion that

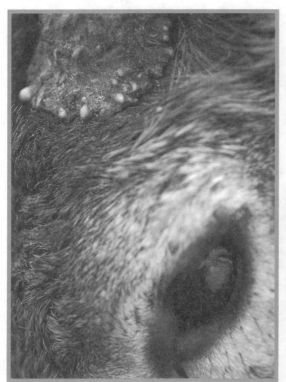

Glands at the base of the antler and around the eye carry each buck's unique scent. This is their main method to communicate with each other. (Courtesy: Susan C. Morse)

A secluded area with plenty of rubs is a good place for a stand.

This is a unique rub. It was made on a brown ash limb that had been cut off by loggers. It was about four feet off the ground.

it's best to keep your understanding of scrapes simple. You don't need to get hung up on science—all you need to know is how to tell a *scrape* from a *pawing*. A pawing is nothing more than a spot where a buck took out some aggression on the ground. It usually doesn't reach bare dirt, and it doesn't have the overhanging limb or droppings found at a scrape. Pawings are prevalent throughout the woods, but they don't mean much except that a buck has traveled through the area, and if you find pawings in a line, you've found a buck's travel corridor.

Scrapes are different. Biologists call them *breeding scrapes* and describe them as places where bucks and does meet for courtship. In some parts of the country that may be true, but from my observations, it doesn't happen that way in the big woods. In twenty years, only once have I seen a doe track around a scrape in the big woods. By the time a doe is ready to breed, a buck will be standing there waiting.

A classic scrape with an overhanging limb. It was made in a hardwood ravine with water running in it. (I call it a wet ravine.)

Bucks impatiently check on the does in their areas, and they're not going to wait around to see if a doe comes to their scrape.

Bucks make scrapes because they are genetically imprinted to do so. They dig all the way to the dirt, urinate, defecate, and then stomp a good hoofprint in them. Often, once this is done, they never freshen the scrape again. They also twist and rub an overhanging limb, which is another calling card to bucks in the area. They leave scent on the limb from the glands around their eyes (the preorbital glands). Periodically they return to a scrape and scent-check the overhanging limb. They'll play with the limb but won't touch the scrape. This tells me that a scrape in the big woods is more for buck-to-buck communication than it is for buck-to-doe communication. Several bucks may use the same scrape if their territories overlap.

Scrapes are great places to ambush bucks. Bucks usually make scrapes on their main travel routes, and it's a sure bet they'll be back to check on them. Furthermore, I believe you can make a buck visit a scrape more often by adding estrous doe scent to it.

SCRAPE + DOE SCENT = SUCCESS

Before the season one year, I had built a ground blind on the side of a ridge where the green growth met the hardwoods. Two trails led out of the green growth and down the mountain. By the second week of the season, a scrape had been opened up on the lower trail about seventy yards from the blind, and the print in the scrape indicated a very good buck. I told Jimmy, one of our hunters, that if he sat there every day, he'd have a good chance of seeing a buck. I suggested that he put some doe scent in the scrape in the morning when he arrived and again before he left in the evening. When he walked in to check the scrape on the third morning, he realized he had forgotten the doe

Jimmy's five-pointer that came down the scrape line made by a bigger buck. Jimmy had been sitting a ground blind and adding doe estrous to a scrape every day.

scent. Disgusted with himself, he went to the blind to settle in for the day. He had just sat down and looked toward the scrape when he saw a buck coming down the run. When the buck stopped at the scrape, Jimmy knew it wasn't the big boy, but it was big enough for him, and he flattened him right where he stood. Jimmy's first Maine buck was a nice, fat five-pointer.

When hunting a scrape you know was made by a good buck, keep in mind that there are sure to be other bucks checking it out. Quite often a lesser buck checks an older buck's scrapes to learn the ropes for the day when he'll take charge of his own area. Scrapes and rubs are the keys to unlocking the mystery of how and where big bucks travel and live. If you can learn to read them, you'll unlock the door to many successful hunts for big-woods bucks. ■

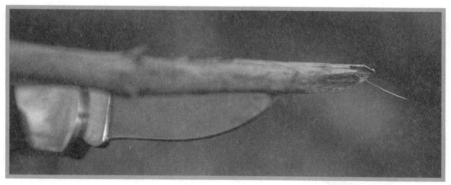

This hair was left on the limb overhanging a scrape as the buck was depositing his scent from his eye and forehead glands. (Courtesy: Susan C. Morse)

The bark from these saplings has been chewed off by rabbits. New hunters in the north woods sometimes mistake them for buck rubs. (Look close for teeth marks in the bark made during snowfall.)

Harold Rose from New Jersey with a
nice big woods buck he shot while
hunting with us at Cedar Ridge.

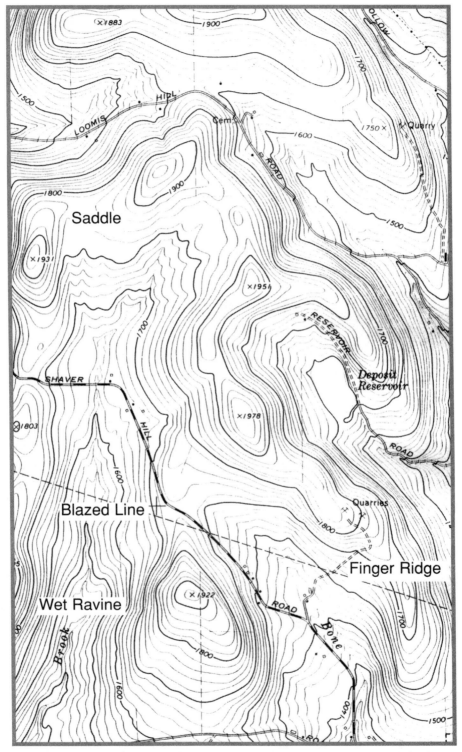

Topo maps are an ideal, and often necessary, tool when hunting big woods bucks.

TAKE A STAND

S tand hunting in In the north woods, stand-hunting can be very effective, but to be successful, you must master the arts of sitting and being patient, and you must find a good place to put your tree stand or ground blind. It takes a certain mindset to keep yourself in one spot, especially if you're not seeing deer. I say this as someone who hasn't mastered the art of either sitting or patience, but I don't intend to worry about them until the day comes when I can't get over the next ridge. I do respect people who *can* sit, though, and I've guided many over the years.

WHERE TO LOCATE YOUR STAND

SCOUTING ON PAPER

Where you put your stand is obviously an important consideration. Let's assume you're heading to the north woods for the first time. Buy some topographical (topo) maps of the area and study them before you go. This will save you some scouting time if you know what kinds of features to look for on the map. Look for ridges—especially long, steep ridges—with saddles through them. Look for wet areas, including lakes, streams, and bogs. Even if you're hunting in relatively flat country, study the higher ground, since that's probably where the hardwoods—and most of the deers' food—will be. Look for ravines or finger ridges that connect the two ravines. Once you've marked these features, find roads or trails that will take you near them.

Now that you've scouted on paper, you're ready to hit the road for some real scouting. Before you take to the woods on foot, drive through the area in your vehicle and check to see if any new roads have been built for logging, since the date on the map. Many topo maps were last updated in the late eighties, and some haven't been updated since the seventies. Update your map by drawing in new roads and features such as clear-cuts that aren't shown on the map.

> ### SUCCESSFUL SCOUTING WITH A TOPO MAP
> When I wanted to change my hunting area in the mid-eighties, the only topo maps available were from the 1920s. A whole forest could have been logged and regrown in that time! I looked over the maps and

found an area I liked. It had a mountain ridge about three miles long with a lake on one side. I had only one day to scout at the site—in early October. I drove in on each side of the mountain as far as I could and then walked farther on overgrown logging roads. The area looked and felt right. It had some big hardwood ridges with green growth up high, and I was encouraged to see a few tracks in the leaves. That fall and the following one I shot nice bucks on that mountain. My topo map scouting had been a success. :●

SCOUTING ON SITE

When you head into the woods to scout, check out the streams first. Streams and other wet areas are good places to find deer signpost rubs as this is where brown ash, a favorite of deer, usually grows. Look for wet deer runs crossing streams at shallow spots or places where the stream banks are low. These are good stand locations because the deer tend to use these runs repeatedly. If there are signposts at a crossing, it's probably an especially good place for a stand.

After you've scouted the streams, work your way up the ridges, checking spring seeps for signposts. If you find a run paralleling the ridge, follow it—there's a good chance it will lead to a passage through the ridge. Also check hardwood ridges for feeding sign (evidence of pawing for ferns or vegetation nipped), especially if you discover fresh droppings. Does usually spend time in places like this, so consider placing your stand near one during the rut. Does in the big woods don't have specific bedding areas. They wander about feeding and then bed at a good vantage point to detect danger. Several bucks may pass through such an area once they start looking for does.

Early May is a good time to scout. The snow has just melted and the leaves haven't come out yet. The woods looks just as they did in late fall. Trails will still be beaten down and scrapes will be easy to spot, even at a distance. Rubs will be fairly bright and strings of bark will still be hanging from them. If you can't scout in May, you might as well wait until late fall, after the leaves are off the trees. During the summer, it's hard to see much with the foliage out, and rubs will have turned gray and started to heal, making them difficult to spot. Personally, I do my scouting about a week before deer-hunting season. The leaves have been down for a week or two, giving the deer time make some tracks. (Scouting in early October is discouraging—as the leaves come raining down, they cover tracks as fast as the deer make them. You might be walking through good deer country and swear there isn't a deer around!)

DON'T BE AFRAID TO COVER SOME GROUND WHEN SCOUTING

When you're scouting for a stand location, don't be afraid to cover a lot of ground. I've seen hunters go into the woods a quarter mile or so and look around a little bit.

The buck that sparred with this beech sapling must have long tines to twist it up this way. (Note the well-worn trail that continues on.)

A typical area where brown ash grows— a wet run through the thick green growth.

If they don't see much sign, they give up and go somewhere else. If you go far enough into the woods and check the streams and ridges, you *will* find buck sign. And you may also find a better way to get to a stand location you're considering.

A SHORT DRAG

Once I was scouting a new area a week before the season, and I had some hunters coming in who wanted to stand-hunt. After going up and down some big hardwood ridges for a couple of miles, I found a spot where bucks were traveling down from a softwood bluff into the hardwoods. I built a ground blind there, realizing that in my travels I had made my way to within half a mile of an old truck road that I could drive to. When I left that spot to work my way out, I hit a deer run. It was going my way, so I followed it.

I came to a place where the trees were torn up with fresh rubs, so I went uphill about fifty yards and built another ground blind. After hiking another hundred yards down the ridge, I came out at the road. What

One of the Massachusetts boys with his high racked seven-pointer taken out of a ground blind overlooking a rub line.

luck—a nice rub line close to a road!

The first day the hunters were there, I walked each one to a blind, but all they saw were a couple of does. The next day they swapped blinds, so I walked them both in again. Only half an hour after I dropped the hunter at the blind closer to the road, he started shooting. I hurried over and found him standing over a beautiful, high-racked seven-pointer. We had a good chuckle about the short drag—we could see the truck from where he shot the deer!

SCOUTING DURING HUNTING SEASON

I do more scouting during hunting season than at any other time. As I still-hunt and when I'm tracking bucks, I frequently learn more in one day about the locations of buck travel corridors, rubs, and other signposts than I do in a week of pre-season scouting. I sometimes end up in areas that are new to me, and I call this connecting the dots, because I sometimes learn where competing bucks' ranges overlap. These overlap areas are great places for stands, because you have a chance to see two bucks instead of just one.

This hunter is prepared to stay on stand as long as it takes, to get his chance at a buck.

THE BEST STAND LOCATIONS

Try to put your stand in one of these three types of locations:

DOE FEEDING AREAS: These are best once the rut kicks in and the bucks change their travel patterns to check on the does.

TRAVEL CORRIDORS: Look for corridors that funnel deer through natural terrain features like shallow stream beds. These are great places for a stand any time during the season,

Travel corridors are often found where a steep ridge levels out.

and you're likely to see many deer near them. Place your stand back from the corridor—where it's easier to watch the whole area without a buck slipping around behind you—in a spot with good wind advantage.

NEAR A SCRAPE LINE OR A RUB LINE: Stands near scrape lines or rub lines work well any time during the season, and if you can find an intersection of two lines, you'll have even better luck. Early in the season, the bucks will be establishing lines. Later, they'll be checking their scrapes and rubs as they make rounds to see if other bucks are horning in on their territory.

A well-worn trail dropping down from a saddle. An ideal stand location.

A SUCCESSFUL BLIND NEAR A CORRIDOR

A travel corridor was about a quarter mile from the tents at one of our remote camps, and deer used it almost daily. The corridor came from a mountain down a finger ridge, crossed a logging road, and then split into smaller trails in a softwood bottom with a stream running through it. One evening I had just returned to camp, and one of the hunters—who had already filled his tag—said he had seen a buck and two does come through the corridor. I ran up to check the tracks and confirmed it was a good buck. It was the peak of the rut, so I figured he'd still be hanging around the does in the morning. The does' tracks led down into

Bill with his 225-pound buck. He took this buck while posted up on a trail that a doe had already gone down. The buck was an eight-pointer, but had broken most of his points off while fighting.

the low ground, so I planned to have the two other hunters, Bob and Bill, there the next day.

When we got to the corridor in the morning, we saw that the three deer had come back across the trail in the night, and the buck had made a scrape in the trail. A little more trail-checking showed us that the does had recently gone back down to the low ground, but the buck hadn't. I told the hunters I thought the buck would be back, and sent Bob down to the rock blind and had Bill post to cover the crossing. I followed the buck's track up the mountain, thinking that if he had bedded up there and I jumped him, he'd come back down. I got up a little way and jumped a buck, but it wasn't the one I was looking for, so I continued on. After a while, I saw that my buck had turned and was heading back toward Bill, following the does' tracks. Just then I heard shooting down below. I hurried along, following the tracks, and soon I could see Bill standing in the trail ahead. When I got down to him, he told me the buck had come right down the ridge and stopped about seventy-five yards from him, so he put the cross hairs on him and fired. The buck took off and cleared the trail as if he hadn't been hit. Bill fired again, and the buck disappeared into the green growth, although Bill didn't think he could have missed. I saw no blood as I followed the running track into the softwood, but after about a hundred yards, there lay Bill's buck, stretched out on top of a blowdown he couldn't make it across. He was a battle-scarred old buck and weighed 225 pounds. He was an eight-pointer, but his antlers had broken off to points flush at the beam from fighting.   :●

ON STAND NEAR A SCRAPE

One year it had been quite warm prior to hunting season, and buck activity was fairly low. As I scouted during the week before the season started, I could not find any good scrapes in the area where I wanted to hunt. I *did* find where a good buck had been sparring with a few trees on a rub line, and I knew there were other bucks in the area, even though the sign didn't indicate it.

Eddie, my hunter that week, had hunted in Maine for three years and had never even seen a buck. This was his first hunt with me, and when he came in on Sunday, I explained that the conditions were not the best, but we were going to make the most of them. He said he didn't care what size buck he shot, he just wanted a Maine buck. Well, Eddie got his first Maine buck on his second day on stand. A nice five-pointer came right down the rub line, checking the big boy's work.

Would Eddie have killed the big boy if he had passed up the five-point?

Eddy's first Maine buck, taken while watching a well-used scrape line.

Who knows. To him the five-pointer was a trophy he had waited four years for. When you're on stand, you never know which buck will show up first, but one thing's for sure—if you scout your stand location well, you'll have a better chance of scoring on a buck than if you just pick any old stump to sit on.

A simple ground blind can be made from dead limbs and small spruce or fir trees.

TREE STAND OR GROUND BLIND?

Once you've found the perfect place for your stand, you have to consider how to spend a week or so there comfortably and still have a good chance of scoring a buck. Tree stands are the most popular way to hunt in most of the whitetail's range. They have advantages, but they also have drawbacks. They are great around grown-up clear-cuts, where you need to see over the new growth, and they're also good around swales and bogs, where the tall

This beech rub was done by a big racked buck. Note how the limb is mangled and twisted. (Courtesy: Susan C. Morse)

grass can hide a deer, or in green growth, where visibility is low and you might need to see behind you.

But tree stands are not so great if you've picked a spot farther out than you want to carry a stand or if you're likely to get antsy sitting in a very limited amount of space for a very long period of time. It's hard to sit for eight or nine hours without stretching or moving around. It can also be extremely cold when the wind is blowing and you're up in a tree with no shelter.

I prefer ground blinds in most situations. I've found very few situations where they don't work. You might think deer smelling your scent would be problem, but it doesn't seem to be, since the wind rarely blows in one direction long enough to carry the scent far. If you use a good cover scent and deer scent, you'll have no problem. I also like ground blinds because I can carry an axe or saw when I scout and make blinds as I find good locations. Also, in a well-made ground blind you'll stay warmer than in a tree stand, because you'll be able to move around, stretch, and be sheltered from the wind.

BUILDING A GROUND BLIND

I find a spot on a ridge looking downhill or with enough thick cover in back of me that a buck can't sneak around behind the blind. I use what's available in the woods. I might start with an uprooted tree or a log. Then I make a frame with small dead logs about as high as my neck will be when I'm sitting down. Next I try to find some spruce boughs to block off the wind and break up the outline of the blind to make it less visible to deer. Then I remove dead twigs and leaves from the floor of the blind so I won't make noise as I move around. I can sit in a place like this for hours. If I need to move around, it's no problem—I can even make a little fire right inside if necessary. You'll be surprised how close deer will come to a ground blind without ever knowing you're there.

A GROUND BLIND NEAR A SCRAPE AND A RUB

A few years ago I built a ground blind in a tangle of spruce blowdowns with a thick stand of spruce behind it. It was so natural-looking that I did very little to camouflage it. Thirty yards in front of it was a good scrape on a rub line leading into a swamp. The first day I put Sean in the blind. He said a six-pointer came to the scrape but never stopped in the opening, so he didn't shoot. I told him that in that mess I doubted whether bucks could *stop* in an opening—he'd have to shoot when they *crossed* an opening. He went back the next day and a spikehorn showed up, but since he wanted the six-pointer he'd seen the day before, he just watched the spike. Pretty soon the spike walked right up to the edge of the blind and tried to look in. Sean sat perfectly still, and after a while the spike went to check out the scrape. It stayed around so long that Sean changed his mind and shot it—his first Maine buck.

SUMMING UP

Stand-hunting is a very effective way to hunt bucks *if* you develop a mindset that keeps you on stand no matter what the weather or what you see (or don't see!). I tell my hunters that it takes only a second for that once-in-a-lifetime buck to show up. If you're prepared for the elements and you've picked an appropriate spot for your blind, you'll have a good chance of a buck showing up while you're there. ∎

This is the Dueling Buck, where
he fell after being grunted back
to me while I was tracking him.

Being able to surprise a mature buck off guard takes skill and patience. Hunters must be prepared to react quickly to a scene like this when stalking or tracking big bucks.

6

Being Prepared

Being prepared is probably the most important aspect of a successful hunt. Physical as well as mental preparation is necessary if you plan to pursue bucks in the big woods. And being in good physical shape is important even if you are a stand-hunter. What if you've found a super spot for a stand and it's a mile back in the woods from the nearest road? Will you be able to get to it in a reasonably short time even if it's halfway up a mountain? Can you get there without breaking out in a wash of sweat? Can you haul your buck out of the woods from your chosen location? A lot of hunters don't think about these things until it's too late, and their hunt is ruined because they've fooled themselves about the condition they're in.

I tell all hunters who want to still-hunt or track to get in shape as if they were going on a sheep hunt. Most of them think I'm crazy, as they're used to walking out to the back forty with no problem, but it's usually easy to tell—within the first hour of the hunt—who paid attention. It's surprising how many hunters think that walking three miles a day down the sidewalk is getting in shape.

LOST OPPORTUNITY

One year during opening week in remote camp, we got the first group of hunters settled in and it started snowing. As usual, this brought camp spirits up especially high. I asked if anyone wanted to try tracking in the morning, and Bruce quickly volunteered. We awoke the next morning to a six-inch blanket of nice, powdery snow—the kind you dream about. We ate breakfast, grabbed our lunches, and headed out as it was getting light. We hadn't gone a hundred yards from the tent when we cut a decent buck track crossing the trail behind camp. I estimated that he was a two-and-a-half-year-old and suggested we look for a better track. Bruce agreed and we headed down the trail. We found what we were looking for when we cut a very good track fifty yards farther down the trail. The wind was blowing and it was still snowing a little, perfect conditions for good tracking. The buck was headed up the mountain, and I told Bruce we had a good chance of killing him before the day was over.

The buck zigzagged back and forth up the mountain. We had tracked him about half a mile when he turned abruptly toward a green knob. I told Bruce to wait on his back track while I made a circle to see if he was still on the knob. I made the decision to circle too late. The buck wasn't on top of the knob—he was lying at the base of it and had seen us approach. He spooked and headed for the top of the mountain. This meant we should have a better chance at him since he was up and moving. I told Bruce we were going to take the track and see what our next move would be. Bruce told me that he had already perspired quite a bit in coming up the mountain as far as we already did. So, I made another circle to see if the buck might have bedded down again. I found no tracks coming out of the thicket, so I knew he was in there somewhere. I made a smaller circle, but when I was closing back around I spooked him again. This time, when he ran out of the thicket he went down his back track. He stayed in his track for about half a mile before leaving it and going over the top of the mountain. All I could think of was what a chance Bruce had missed because he wasn't in shape and wasn't able to keep up.

GET IN SHAPE PHYSICALLY

The two most important things to work on are your legs and your wind. There are a lot of ways to do this. An obvious one is to do some mountain climbing in the summer. For most people, though, that is not practical, so going to a gym is another solution. Work out on a treadmill or stair-climbing machine, or simply walk up and down stairs. Try going up a twenty-story building using the stairs and you'll get a feel for what kind of shape you're in. Riding a bicycle is another great way to get in shape, especially if you're in an area that has some hills. Bicycling builds your legs as well as your wind.

BEING IN SHAPE MEANS BEING SUCCESSFUL

Thanksgiving week one year I was guiding Todd, a young hunter from Pennsylvania who wanted to learn how to track. The first morning of the hunt there was about a foot of snow on the ground and the weather had warmed up enough to start melting it. We picked up a good buck track high on a ridge. The buck was heading down the ridge, checking for does as he went. He led us into an old, tangled-up chopping, where he crossed another good buck track. The second track was fresher, so I opted to start following that one. We followed the new buck into a huge fir thicket. Since his track was fresh, I thought he might have just started making his rounds. I learned that I had guessed wrong when we found

Todd's big ten-pointer. I took Todd on a fast-paced tracking job through every beaver bog in the area.

his fresh bed and a set of running tracks leaving it. We pushed our way out of the thicket and sat down to eat a sandwich while we waited for the buck to settle down. When we returned to the track, I noticed there was something odd about it—the buck had a bum foot. Every so often there was a drag mark in the snow with a little blood in it.

The buck stayed in the thickest cover he could find, and I knew he was going to be a tough one to kill. I told Todd that if he was up to it, I thought we could press him enough to get a shot at him. Todd said he was up to it, and off we went. I set the pace at a fast walk and never let up. We jumped the buck five times without giving him any time for the rest he needed to run on three legs. He led us through every beaver bog and stream in the area trying to lose us. It was getting late and we were a few miles from the truck when the buck crossed a big bog and then ran down an old truck road. He stayed on the road for half a mile, trying to gain some ground on us. We pressed on, trying to close the gap. He turned off the road and into another thicket. I looked ahead and could see another bog out in front of us. I hurried to the edge to look across and saw nothing. I turned to see how Todd was doing, and when I looked back into the bog, I could see the buck running for the other side. I said, "He's right there," and I jumped aside to let Todd shoot. On his third shot I saw the buck drop out of sight into the swale grass. I congratulated Todd on his good shooting, and we headed across the bog to find the buck. On the way, I discovered why I had not seen him at first. He had gone into the brook, was wading down it, and was below the level of the brush. We crossed the brook and found Todd's buck, a beautiful ten-pointer. I checked his legs to see which one was injured and found he had cut a front ankle right through the tendons and couldn't use it. No doubt we saved that buck from a slow death by coyotes.

If Todd had not been in the shape he was, I doubt that he would have shot that buck. Todd told me he raced mountain bikes to keep in shape. He was also familiar with his gun and practiced with it enough to be able to make a shot when it counted. Being in shape can make the difference between being successful or not, and it's up you to decide if you want to be in shape.

GET IN SHAPE MENTALLY

Mental preparation is also very important. I've seen hunters defeat themselves because they weren't prepared to accept the fact that hunting might be hard. In the big woods, if you see six or eight deer in a week, it's a good week. I've guided hunters who saw twenty deer in a week, and I've guided hunters who saw none. I've observed that the hunters who see the most deer are the ones who hunt all week without getting discouraged. They roll with the punches, understanding that many variables can influence the outcome of a hunt. If you can master patience and persistence, everything else will fall into line. If you can't, you'll have a tough time, because you'll be easily discouraged.

Eddy's second Maine buck. Eddie took this buck the last day of his hunt after sitting all week watching a scrape that he was freshening with doe estrus.

PERSISTENCE PAYS OFF

Once I guided Eddie, a hunter who wanted only to stand-hunt and was prepared to do whatever it took to be successful. I had found a fresh scrape along a travel corridor way back on the side of a mountain. Eddie was game to sit there. It was a mile-and-a-half walk on an old winter road. Eddie carried a pack containing his lunch, extra clothes, and a seat cushion. Every day he headed to his stand before daylight and came out at dark. He put doe scent in the scrape morning and evening. Halfway through the week his feet hurt from walking in his heavy boots, but that didn't matter to Eddie. He simply switched to some lighter boots and carried his heavy ones. By Friday evening he had not seen one deer, but he didn't complain. He asked me if I thought he should go back for the last day. I told him he should, since he had already put in so much time. He went back in the next morning and killed a five-point buck that came to check the scrape.

Very few hunters hang in like Eddie did. They talk themselves out of their spot for one reason or another. Learning to have patience and persistence is the key to your success. For me, learning to be patient has been a long battle. I spent a lot of years bumbling around spooking bucks before I realized I was going to have to learn to be patient. When I finally did, it changed the way I hunted and made me more successful. But it's still something I'm working on.

BE PREPARED FOR THE UNEXPECTED—AND THE EXPECTED

Be prepared to stay in the woods overnight. Hopefully you'll never have to, but if the occasion arises, you need to know what to do. I have never had to spend a night in the woods while deer hunting, but I'm prepared to, and Deb knows it, so she won't panic if I don't return on time. You can spend the night reasonably comfortably if you carry a few basic items in your pack: a space blanket, some rope for dragging, some candy bars, and something to start a fire with.

Once you realize you're not going to make it out of the woods—because you didn't figure your time right or you twisted an ankle—it's time to prepare for the night. First, gather some dry firewood—about three times as much as you think you'll need for the night. Build a fire against a big tree or log to deflect the heat toward you. Then make a lean-to by tying a fallen young tree between two trees and leaning some other poles against it. Cover the poles with spruce or fir boughs to shelter you from the wind. Then make a thick mat of boughs to lie on. With a small fire and your lean-to three or four feet away from it, you can wrap up in your space blanket and be warm and cozy.

Be prepared to make a shot when you have the opportunity. Be familiar enough with your gun to be able to make a quick shot. I've had hunters come into camp with brand-new rifles they haven't even practiced with. Make sure your gun is sighted in. I like to sight my rifle to hit one inch high at fifty yards. This gives me a dead-on hold at any range I'm able to shoot. If you traveled far to get to your hunting site, especially if you traveled by air, check to see if your gun is still sighted in. Don't blow the opportunity to shoot a once-in-a-lifetime buck because you didn't take that extra minute to check it out.

READY, AIM, FIRE!

I was still-hunting back to camp with Dana late one afternoon. We had been hunting for four days and hadn't seen a decent buck. We were still half a mile from camp, and I was setting a pretty good pace so we'd make it back before dark. We headed up a steep ridge, and when I stopped halfway up for Dana to catch his breath, I heard footsteps shuffling along over a knoll to our left. As the sound got closer I told Dana to get ready, because it sounded like a buck dragging his feet. When the buck came over the knoll, he was below us, and all we could see was his rack. As he went behind a blowdown I realized there would be only one chance for a shot. I told Dana to aim between two trees and grabbed my grunt call, thinking I might be able to stop him in the opening. I needn't have bothered—as soon as the buck hit the opening, Dana fired and dropped him in his tracks. We walked down to find a perfectly symmetrical ten-pointer. Dana was familiar with his rifle and had practiced enough to get the job done.　　　◗

Dana's perfectly symmetrical ten-pointer. Dana took this buck while still-hunting a hub area of signpost rubs.

I call this the two-jump shot. I get my rifle lined up and ready when the buck crosses the first opening.

RUNNING SHOTS

There's a lot of controversy about taking shots at running deer. Some people say that if a deer is running, you can't be sure whether your bullet is going in a safe direction. Others say that if a deer is running you can't be sure of hitting your target. I think it boils down to personal choice. I will say this, though: If you don't learn to make running shots, you may not get many shots at big-woods bucks. Over the years, I've taken a lot of bucks that were running, and I've never wounded one—either I've made a good shot or I've had a clean miss. With enough practice you can become proficient at making running shots. I call my method the *two-jump shot*. When a buck makes a jump where I can see him, I line up on his direction of travel. By the time he jumps again, I'm swinging with him, and I fire when my bead is on his shoulder. If he's running in heavy cover, I swing with him, scanning for an opening he will enter, and I shoot when he hits the opening. I always aim right on the buck; I don't aim ahead of him (lead him). In close range there's no reason to lead a buck as long as you maintain your swing with him.

A good way to practice your running shots is to put a piece of cardboard or wood in the center of an automobile tire, have a buddy roll it down a hill, and try to shoot it. If It's a bumpy hill, all the better, as it will mimic the movement of a jumping buck.

Being prepared will save you a lot of frustration and will allow you to enjoy your hunt more, because you'll be capable of doing whatever it takes when pursuing a buck. Being prepared is an ongoing process, so have fun with it. Make it a team effort with your hunting buddies, and enjoy your successes together. ■

Seasoned deer hunter Kate Fiduccia plans the best downwind approach to stalk a deep narrow ridge known to harbor big bucks. (Courtesy: Fiduccia Enterprises)

GEARING UP

Being prepared is probably the most important aspect of a successful hunt. Physical as well as mental preparation is necessary if you plan to t is essential for you to wear proper clothing so that you can stay warm and comfortable during a long day in the woods. If you're hunting in the big woods, be prepared for drastic and rapid weather changes. I've seen weather change from rain to snow, and from calm to gale-force winds in an hour. If you dress properly, these kinds of changes shouldn't be a problem. Base what you wear on how you'll be hunting.

STAND-HUNTING

Stand-hunters have a little more flexibility in the way they dress than do still-hunters. Since most of the time you'll be staying still rather than moving around, you'll need warm clothes, so carry a pack with extra clothing. On your way to the stand, you may want to carry some of your outerwear rather than wear it so that you don't work up a sweat by the time you reach your site. There are many new fabrics and insulations on the market today, but I have yet to see any that is better than wool in all aspects. Some of the new synthetic materials have advantages, but they also have disadvantages. The hunters I've guided over the years have tested many types of clothing, and what seems to work best for stand-hunters is wearing layers of clothing. Start out with wool blend or polypropylene long underwear. Over that pull on light wool pants and shirt and then a heavy wool sweater or vest. Top it all off with Thinsulate®–lined fleece jacket and pants, which are lightweight and can be carried to your stand and used when you need them. Wear wool socks and boots with removable insulated liners and wool mittens that flip back to expose your fingers—they'll keep your hands warm even if they get wet. A warm hat with ear flaps is a must, and you may want to consider a face mask. Carry a light rain suit if the day might turn soggy. Dressed like this you should have no problem staying warm on stand no matter what the weather does.

STILL-HUNTING OR TRACKING

I dress the same whether I'm still-hunting or tracking, and the way I dress, I'm comfortable whether it's ten degrees or fifty degrees. This way I don't have to bother carrying extra clothes or shedding clothes that I'd have to carry. I wear wool-blend

This is the clothing I wear most every day of the season. The only exception is the sweater on the left is only worn when the temperature drops to near zero.

long underwear top and bottom. For pants I prefer Filson wool, as they wear like iron and repel water. I use suspenders, since wool pants can be heavy when wet. On top I wear a medium-weight wool shirt and over that a green plaid wool cape-back jackshirt. It has a zipper, a doubled wool shoulder cap, and no lining. I wear eighteen-inch-high ankle-fit uninsulated rubber boots over one pair of heavy wool socks. A baseball-type cap keeps the sun and blowing snow out of my eyes. If it's cold enough, I wear wool gloves—the kind with the rubber dot grips. The only time I change this clothing combination is if it is extremely cold or warm. When it's cold I'll trade the uninsulated boots for the same kind insulated, and I may add a sweater and a hat with earflaps. If it's warm, I opt for a pair of light wool pants and don't wear the jackshirt. Dressed like this I'm very rarely uncomfortable.

WOOL IS THE BEST CHOICE

As you can see, I'm adamant about wearing wool. I tell hunters booking one-on-one hunts to bring wool, but invariably some show up with the newest clothes they've seen advertised. As I said before, I've tested them all, and my conclusion is that nothing breathes, sheds water, stays quiet, and keeps you warm when it's wet like wool does. Fleece is the second choice, but it wets through quickly and then fails to keep you warm. Gore-Tex fabric is much too noisy when you're moving around. Although some fabrics feel quiet to the touch, most are very noisy when you're going through brush.

When hunters show up with the newest synthetic products, I tell them we'll give their clothes a test. Usually after the first day they say they wished they had listened and brought wool. Most of the pants they bring are stiff, and every little limb that slaps against them makes a loud pop. There's no way to get near a buck making that kind of noise.

Probably the worst fabric you can wear is cotton. Cotton against your body will keep you cold and clammy if you sweat. It absorbs water like a sponge, and when it's wet it will sap the heat from your body. I will not guide anyone wearing cotton clothes, as I feel I would be endangering them by doing so. We have a saying in deer camp: *Cotton is death, so wear your woollies.*

CHOOSING A RIFLE

Once you choose your clothing, you'll need to decide what type of rifle to use. Whatever type you pick, become comfortable and familiar with it before you go hunting—you don't want to fumble with the safety if you need to make a quick shot, and you want to be able to work the action quickly to make a second shot. Consider weight if you'll be walking any distance. Stand-hunters don't have to worry about this as much as still-hunters or trackers, but if you're stand-hunting, you *do* need to have a good scope to help you see the saplings and branches through which you may have to pick an opening. A low- to medium-power scope is best. Your stand location may give you a thirty-yard shot, but shots beyond a hundred yards are rare unless you're hunting around clear-cuts.

For tracking or still-hunting, you'll want a light, fast-handling rifle. A pump or lever-action carbine is the best choice for several reasons: they're short, they're light, and they balance well. These qualities are critical if you'll be carrying your rifle all day up mountains and through thick brush. Pumps and levers also have fewer problems in snowy and icy conditions.

Over the years I've tried bolt actions, semi-autos, and lever actions in all types of weather and conditions. They all had some advantages and some disadvantages. I finally settled on a Remington 7600 carbine pump, in .30-06. I like its light, fast handling, smooth action, balance and feel of it. I use a Williams receiver sight that screws on the rear scope-mount holes. I brushed fluorescent orange paint on the bead and sealed it with clear fingernail polish to make the bead stand out on bare ground or snow. I don't use a sling—it's just something else to catch in the brush. The only reason I can think of for using a sling is so you can have both hands free for dragging out your buck. I carry a short piece of nylon rope with a slipknot at each end to use as a gun sling. I stretch a piece of electrical tape over the end of the barrel to keep out rain or snow and wrap extra tape around the barrel to use in case I fire a shot. (I learned this trick from one of my guides who also works in Alaska.)

My standard equipment. Depending on where I'm hunting I might add a topo map and GPS.

WHAT YOU NEED TO CARRY AND WHAT YOU DON'T

So many gadgets on the market today claim to be the answer to bagging a big buck that I don't know how a new hunter can sort them all out. Too many hunters spend more time trying them than they do hunting! Most of these gadgets are a new twist on an old idea. Keep in mind they all add weight and take up space in your pack, and an extra pound will feel like five by the end of the day.

MUST-HAVE ITEMS

Besides your rifle, ammunition, and clothing, here's what I feel is necessary to carry and why. Pack these things and then decide whether you need anything else.

Binoculars. Since my rifle has no scope, I carry binoculars. I have a pair of Nikon 10x40 that weighs eighteen ounces. I carry them around my neck inside my jacket and take them out only if I catch a movement or see something out of place that I can't identify. Often it turns out to be a deer.

HIDDEN DEER DISCOVERED BY BINOCULARS

I was guiding Mike, and we were tracking a buck that was with a doe and lamb. They began wandering and feeding their way up a ridge. We eased over the top and saw that the tracks led out into a flat area that was full of winter beech—the kind that carry their dead leaves all winter. I used my binoculars to look at an odd shade of brown among the leaves. Just as I focused on the spot, I saw that it was a deer, and it was coming toward us. Mike was off to my right twenty yards, and I told him not to move. A few minutes later the doe and lamb had fed their way back to within thirty yards of us, and I knew the buck wouldn't be far behind. Sure enough, a nice ten-pointer came out of the beeches looking for his doe. Mike's .30-06 roared and it was the end of the story for the old boy.

If I hadn't had my binoculars, it's doubtful that I would have seen the deer. Mike's glad I had them along that day.

Compass. Carrying a compass and knowing how to use it are critical. If you end up in a thick swamp or in a snowstorm, you'll almost certainly walk in circles if you don't use one. Many hunters use the ball-type compasses they can pin on their jacket. These are fine for knowing which general direction you're headed, but

Mike's ten-pointer, taken a quarter mile from where we picked up his track. I picked him out with binoculars as he stood in the brown leaves of a winter beech grove.

they're useless if you're using a map to keep tabs on where you are. I recommend using a flat-sided compass with a movable bezel. Learn to use it in conjunction with a map and you'll save yourself a lot of time and headaches. Having a compass is so important that I always carry two—one in my pocket and one in my belt pack. There's always the possibility of losing one, and if you doubt the direction one compass is pointing, you can double-check it with the other.

Map. If I'm hunting an unfamiliar area, I always carry a map. It helps me to find the easiest way around terrain features and out of the woods at the end of the day.

Disposable lighter and matches in a waterproof container. I carry both for insurance.

Space blanket. It will help you keep warm and dry if you have to spend the night in the woods, and it's protection if you get caught in torrential rain.

Quarter-inch nylon rope for dragging your deer and slinging your rifle.

Knife. Use it for field dressing your buck or anything else you need to cut. A five-inch blade is plenty long.

Food. Take lunch and extra chocolate or protein bars in case you have a long walk or drag out of the woods.

Water. If you are not familiar with the quality of stream or creek water in the area you are hunting, be sure to carry some bottled water with you.

OPTIONAL ITEMS

These are some other items I carry. You'll have your own preferences according to the way you hunt.

Deer calls. I wear a grunt tube around my neck and carry a snort call in my pocket.

Buck scent. I spray it on my sleeves and pant legs.

GPS (global positioning system). I use it to mark points of interest.

35mm camera. This allows me to get good-quality photos of trophies. I use a camera with a timer so I can be in the picture even if I'm hunting alone.

Pack. Depending on how you'll be hunting, choose between a belt pack and a backpack. A belt pack is more suited for still-hunting and tracking, because you'll be ducking under low limbs and blowdowns, sometimes on your hands and knees. A backpack will catch on branches and snap them off. I like a belt pack made of fleece without a lot of extra pouches. I wear it under my jacket so snow doesn't build up on it. If you're stand-hunting, you'll probably want to use a backpack or day pack because you'll need room to carry extra clothes and maybe a thermos filled with something hot to drink.

Proper clothing is essential to being comfortable enough to stay afield all day and enjoy your hunt. Proper equipment is essential to the safety and success of your hunt. Choose quality equipment and take care of it, and it will give you many seasons of use. ■

When spending long hours in the deep woods stalking a buck, it is important to be dressed properly. All your gear should be lightweight and durable. The C.C. Filson backpack will stand up to the toughest conditions. (Courtesy: Fiduccia Enterprises)

Even on bare ground, it's easy to see where this buck is traveling. A monster buck made this scrape and the huge rub on the spruce behind it.

STILL-HUNT AT A VARIABLE PACE

ecoming a successful still-hunter is a very rewarding accomplishment. Still-hunting for deer in the big woods dates back to a time when Native Americans quietly moved through the forest in buckskin clothing trying to get within bow range of the animals so they could kill them and feed their families. Their whole existence depended on their hunting ability. Today, even with modern firearms, it's still the challenge of man against beast that lures us to the woods each season. Still-hunting requires a combination of stealth, patience, and knowledge of the whitetail's habits and habitat. Still-hunting pits man against deer in the game of hide and seek. When you still-hunt for a big buck, you have to become a part of his environment. To be successful, you have to think like a buck so you can put yourself where he is. A still-hunter must be able to adapt to ever-changing forest conditions. If you hunt the big woods, whether in the Adirondacks or New Brunswick, you must realize that these areas have low deer densities and you may have to travel a long distance to find one.

Mike Featherstone with his wide-beamed nine-point buck taken on a remote hunt with Cedar Ridge Outfitters. Mike's success was directly related to knowing when to pick up the pace and when to slow down while following the buck's tracks.

HUNTING THE SIGN

When I still-hunt, I always hunt the sign—that is, I set my pace according to the deer sign I find as I move along. If I see very few tracks or droppings, I move through the area fairly quickly. Once I start seeing sign, whether it's droppings, a scrape, or a rub, I'll slow down and start to analyze what I'm seeing. Of course, I'm always looking for buck sign. The way scrapes and rubs are laid out in an area tells me a lot. Signpost rubs determine my still-hunting route. I hunt slowly around these areas, hoping to catch a buck making his rounds.

HUNTING THE SIGNPOST ROUTE

When hunting at one of my remote camps one year, I routinely hunted one of these signpost routes. The first signpost rub was about half a mile from camp at the base of a hardwood ridge about a hundred yards from a stream. It was the best place to cross the stream, so we usually passed that rub going to and from camp every day. In two weeks of hunting we saw three bucks within fifty yards of the rub. Two were big; one we shot and the other got away. The third was a four-pointer we let go for another year. When you hunt where the sign is, your odds increase tremendously.

HUNTING THE RIDGES AND MOUNTAINS

When hunting in country that has ridges or mountains, spend most of your still-hunting time high up. There are two reasons for this. First, bucks bed high the majority of the time in this type of terrain. Second, when you still-hunt high up, you have the advantage of being able to see better by looking down from above. Bucks feel more secure when bedded high and do not expect danger from above. Often they lie on a bluff overlooking their back track. If the wind is at their back, they can detect danger from behind. Usually a buck will bed in the green growth on top of a ridge or where the green growth meets the hardwoods. The only way to approach a buck bedded like this is to sneak through the green growth, peering over the bluffs and knolls, hoping to catch him bedded or get close enough for a running shot should you jump him.

LESSONS FOR THE HUNTER AND THE HUNTED

One year the first week of the season was especially warm. I was guiding Sue Morse that week, and we hadn't seen as many deer as we usually did. The last day of the hunt we were still-hunting around a mountain where the green growth meets the hardwood. It was another warm, sunny day with leaves crunching underfoot—the kind of day that makes it easy for a hunter to get discouraged. We hadn't see any deer that morning, so we stopped for a sandwich at about eleven o'clock and then decided to continue around the mountain for the afternoon hunt. We eased along as quietly as possible, using the green growth for cover and looking out into a hardwood chopping. We had covered only about a hundred yards when I looked across a ravine and spotted a buck bedded on a ledge under some fir trees, staring in our direction. He was a beautiful eight-pointer with heavy beams and tall points. He was about eighty yards away, and he looked like a statue lying there. Sue brought her gun up and fired. To my amazement, he never moved. She levered another shell and fired again. This time he jumped up and bounded off. We walked over to check for sign of a hit. I found where the bullets had kicked up dirt underneath where he had been, and I knew he wasn't hit.

Sue was using an old octagon-barrel Winchester .30-30 her grandfather had given her, and we discovered that the flip-up peep sight wouldn't lock. It had tipped forward, causing the rifle to shoot low. That was an expensive lesson in checking equipment, and I think that was the day Sue retired her nostalgic old weapon.

That old buck felt secure bedded where he could look down the ravine. He had fir trees behind him for cover so he wouldn't be seen by anything approaching from that direction. If something did approach from behind, all he had to do was make one jump into the ravine and disappear. I'm sure he must have heard us walking in the leaves, but I'm convinced he thought we were other deer. When we got to his bed and looked back, we found that the sun must have been in his eyes and he couldn't see us behind the screen of green growth. The hunter and hunted all became a little wiser that day.

Checking out a scrape with an overhanging limb. (Courtesy: Susan C. Morse)

HUNTING FLAT OR DENSELY FORESTED COUNTRY

If you're hunting in country that is low, flat, and swampy or is heavily forested with evergreens, use different still-hunting tactics. In these areas deer tend to travel more on runs because the woods are usually quite thick. Some of these areas are where deer spend the winter, and they'll have well-worn trails. If this is the case, the best way to still-hunt is to walk these trails. They'll follow the easiest route and are quiet to walk in, since the ground has been packed down from years of use. Move slowly and spend a lot of time looking around. Rely on your eyes—chances are when you see a deer it will be close. You never know when you might meet a big buck coming down the trail toward you. When I guide hunters that want to still-hunt, I send them into this type of area with the confidence that they'll be able to see deer on their own.

ONE THAT GOT AWAY

One year at remote camp, we had planned on hunting a new area the first week of the season. Before the season my other guide, Fred, and I had made some ground blinds in and around a thick tangle of spruce surrounding a huge cedar bog. When we headed down to hunt this area for the first time, all the hunters agreed to take a stand except one. Larry said he couldn't sit still for five minutes and wanted to still-hunt. I sent him into the cedar bog with instructions to stay on the deer trails and move slowly. Later that morning I heard a single shot ring out of the bog. I knew it had to be Larry, but there were no signal shots. That evening, after everyone had gathered back at camp, Larry told us his story. He had been walking a trail that led him into a thick patch of cedars. He pushed his way through the thicket, and when he broke out on the other side, standing there in the trail facing him was a monster buck thirty yards away. Larry said he had never seen antlers that big before. Just as he put up his rifle to shoot, the buck whirled and high-tailed it back where he had come from. Larry had time for one quick shot, but he never touched a hair on that buck.

FOLLOWING THE TRAILS

The first year I guided a remote deer hunt, I booked hunters for the last two weeks of the season. We arrived in camp with the first group on Sunday afternoon of the third week. Everyone had high expectations, since they were the first hunters in this area and six inches of soft snow covered the ground. Of the five hunters, only one wanted to take a stand; the rest wanted to still-hunt or track. They all agreed to post up for a while the first morning to give us guides some time to figure

Rob's 150-class ten-pointer. Rob shot this buck while still hunting along a well-worn deer trail.

things out. Guide Fred found a beaten-down trail through the spruces in an area around a small pond. He went back and told Rob to still-hunt in the trail. Rob followed the trail to where it crossed a logging road and then up a hardwood ridge. As he worked his way up the ridge, a doe came running down the trail and veered off. When he looked back up the trail, he saw a four-pointer coming along the doe's track. He tried to get off a shot but never had a good chance. He was kicking himself about it when he heard a snap and looked up to see a monster buck bringing up the rear. He was trying a running shot when the buck suddenly stopped and gave Rob a broad side. Rob made the shot good and had himself a nice ten-point buck.

That night at camp we compared notes about the deer sign we had found. George, the oldest hunter in camp, said he had found an area he liked and would hunt there again the next day. He described trails criss-crossing through an area of spruce knolls. Late the next afternoon, as all the hunters were drifting back to camp, we heard two shots several hundred yards away. We waited for signal shots, but there were none. One of the hunters decided to go up the trail and check it out anyway. Five minutes later we heard signal shots. We all headed up the trail to see what had happened. When we got to him, George had a ten-pointer lying there that looked like the brother of Rob's buck. He said he was still-hunting the trail out of the thicket, and when he looked ahead of him up the ridge, he could see a deer standing in the trail. He didn't know whether it was a buck or a doe, so he waited. When the deer turned to run, George saw antlers and fired. The buck didn't made it thirty yards before piling up. When we asked George why he hadn't signaled, he said he had carried only three shells, so after he had fired two at the buck, he didn't have two to signal with! :●

WALKING THE TRAILS—SILENTLY

Walking trails is a great way to still-hunt. If you're a new hunter, you'll find it easy to stay where the deer are traveling and you'll be able to walk more quietly if you stay on the trails. When you walk trails in thick cover, you shouldn't have to go too far to get near deer because you'll be in the areas they like to use for cover. Be alert at all times when you hunt these areas. It doesn't take long for a buck to disappear when the visibility is fifty yards or less. This type of hunting requires that you pay more attention to the wind as you travel. Stop, look, and listen often, as you are on the buck's turf, trying to fit into his world.

The "still" in still-hunting has two meanings: to move slowly and to be quiet. Sometimes, though, conditions in the woods are not conducive to moving about silently. It would be nice if every day you hunted there was a carpet of fresh snow— or at least damp leaves—on the ground, but that won't always happen. In reality, you'll hunt a good part of the time in dry, frozen leaves that crunch underfoot. It's important to be able to use whatever conditions you have to your best advantage and realize that there are pluses and minuses to all kinds of conditions.

Hunters who choose not to track when there's snow on the ground always have

George (left) took this wide racked ten-pointer, while still-hunting on a deer trail.

the option to still-hunt. I often still-hunt as I look for a particular track to follow. To me it's much more rewarding than if I were just riding the roads looking for a track. It's not unusual for me to change from tracking to still-hunting in the course of a single day. Still-hunting in the snow is exciting, because your chances of seeing deer increase. You can tell whether you're around deer by the number of tracks, and the deer stand out like beacons on the backdrop of snow. One thing to remember, of course, is that *you* also stand out on the snow. For this reason it's important to use the available cover to your advantage. Skirt around the edges of hardwood openings instead of walking right through the middle of them. If you have to cross an opening, stop often and

If you still hunt on a run like this your chances of seeing a buck are greatly increased. (Courtesy: Susan C. Morse)

look as far as you can in the distance. Deer can detect distant movement on the snow. Your eyes are your most valuable asset when still-hunting in quiet snow. In this game of hide-and-seek, the winner will be the first one to spot the other. If you're the loser, the only sounds you may hear are brush-cracking and deer-snorting. If you're the winner, you may peek around a bush and see a buck lying or standing there with no idea he's in any danger.

BE QUIET—OR ELSE

Craig and I were still-hunting back to camp. We'd been tracking a buck all day and decided to leave him when he turned west and camp was to the east. We were about three miles from camp and it was going to be dark in an hour, so we were moving right along. When we came to a spruce ridge with a steep ravine on the other side, I told Craig to wait while I looked for a place to get down the other side. As I eased out along the edge of the bluff, I noticed where a good buck had milled around during the night. The track lead down into the ravine, so as I neared the edge I kept looking down. I spotted the buck lying on a little knoll in the ravine, about seventy-five yards away. He was facing toward me looking up his back track, but he didn't see me. He had an exceptionally wide rack, and I knew we wanted him. Craig was just out of sight from me, so I gave a light whistle. He started toward me but made no effort to be quiet. When he snapped a couple of sticks, the buck stood up and looked our way. As Craig came out of the firs, I tried to motion for him to stop. He didn't notice me, and after he took a few more steps, the buck turned and sailed away toward the other side of the mountain. That was a tough lesson for Craig. He learned about the need to be as quiet as possible at all times, as the buck of a lifetime can be just around the corner.

SUCCESSFUL STILL-HUNTING

Another time I was still-hunting along a ridge in some choppings during the last week of November when the rut was in full swing. There were tracks of bucks chasing does everywhere. I figured I'd be better off sneaking around trying to catch a buck chasing instead of trying to unravel the spider web of tracks. I worked my way along a shelf for a while, then dropped down into a ravine where I found tracks that were only hours old. As I followed a skid trail through some thick firs, two does jumped into the trail and stopped in it about seventy-five yards away. I could see only one of them, and she began to feed on raspberry stems. I noticed that she kept looking up the ridge where I couldn't see. I thought there just might be a buck up there getting her attention. I waited for a few minutes and tried grunting. I waited another fifteen minutes and still couldn't see anything, but the doe kept looking in the same direction, so I eased ahead, looking where she was looking. All at once I saw a rack coming up out of the brush as the buck bolted down-hill toward the doe. All I could see were flicks of brown, and I couldn't get a shot. Then it dawned on me that the buck was going to cross the

The buck I call Pretty Boy. I shot this eight-point 203-pound buck after a doe tipped me off to his location while I watched her feed.

skid trail I was standing in! I swung my rifle as he moved, and when he jumped into the skid trail, I let fly with two shots before he disappeared over the ridge. I ran to the bottom just in time to see him make his last jump before piling up. He was a nice two hundred-pound eight-pointer.

When there's snow on the ground, tracking isn't the only way to hunt. A patient still-hunter who takes the time to read the sign can be very successful.

TRICKS FOR STILL-HUNTING IN CRUSTED SNOW

Days that warm to above freezing or rain followed by cold nights often cause a crust to form on early-season snow. This is probably the most discouraging condition to still-hunt in. Every step you take sends a signal to every creature in the woods that danger may be approaching. Combine that with the fact that you stand out on the snow, and the odds are definitely against you. Don't throw in the towel, though, as there are ways to capitalize on this condition. Remember, deer will also make a lot of noise when they walk in the crust. The key is to hear them first. To do this you'll have to spend more time standing and listening than walking around. Deer don't like to travel much in the crust, so when you locate fresh tracks, a deer may be close by. You won't get too close to one if he's bedded, but if you hunt with a partner and one of you spooks a deer, the other has a chance of hearing it and getting into a position to shoot. When you're traveling through the woods trying to locate deer, don't try to sneak in crusty snow. To the deer you'll sound like a predator, and they'll be gone before you see them. Instead, move along at a steady pace, stopping every fifty yards or so depending on the terrain. Look around, but mostly listen, as it's surprising how far away you can hear footsteps. This is the way deer travel, and they just might think you're another deer approaching. By keeping in good cover, I have walked surprisingly close to deer before they sensed something was amiss. I've also spotted a deer in the distance that I knew was not going to move my way. When this happened I ran at an angle not directly toward it until I was close enough to tell whether it was a buck. To a deer, this sounds more like another deer than a hunter. By combining any of these tricks with a call, you'll increase your chances of making them work.

So don't hang around camp when the snow is crusty and all the other hunters are discouraged. Get out and enjoy the woods and the hunt. Every day is a new learning experience. Don't be afraid to try something new. I always say, *if you try something enough, something will work, but if you try nothing, nothing will work.*

STILL-HUNTING WITH NO SNOW

I do most of my still-hunting when there is no snow for tracking. With plenty of practice, you can get good at it and be successful. If there's no snow, the best you can hope for is rain-soaked leaves—you'll be able to slip along as quietly as a

7

mouse in a cotton factory. This is when you'll really have to use your eyes. The deer blend in perfectly with their surroundings, and they are silent like ghosts. The only sound you might hear is the thump of their hooves hitting the ground when you spook them. These are the kinds of days when you can get close to deer before being detected. On such days my favorite places to hunt are ones with lots of bluffs and knolls where I can sneak up and peek over the top. I can't tell you how many deer I've seen over the years hunting like this.

Sometimes wet leaves freeze and become crunchy, but they may be that way only for the morning, and then as the day warms, they thaw and become quiet once more. With enough sun, though, they may dry out completely, and then you might as well be walking in cornflakes. If this happens, use the same tactics as you would in crusty snow. Another silent technique is to walk on downed logs or step on rocks when you get the chance. This will help you to cover ground with as little noise as possible.

I hunt an area with three- or four-year-old choppings. Skid trails crisscross the whole mountain. Some of them cut through the green growth almost to the top. It's a perfect place to still-hunt in noisy conditions. I can start from the road in the morning and hunt all day without having to leave a skid trail. Some of these trails that go through the thicker areas have developed into deer trails, making the hunting even better.

The first hunter I took into this area was Sue Morse. It was the first week of the season and we had bare ground, mostly with dry leaves, the whole time. We still-hunted the skid trails all week and saw seventeen deer, four of them good-racked bucks. As luck would have it, though, I couldn't get Sue in position for a shot at any of them. I've been hunting in that area ever since, and it's a rare day when I don't see deer.

TRAIN YOURSELF TO RECOGNIZE SOUNDS

When you're still-hunting, you have to train yourself to hear the sounds around you as you walk. If the leaves are crunchy, most people tend to hear their own footsteps, but you can train your mind to block out the close sounds and concentrate on the distant ones. To be successful, you have to hear and identify the sounds around you. Some sounds, such as a deer snorting, may seem obvious, but a raven can make a similar sound. Stop and listen to make sure it's a deer. Other sounds are subtle, and you may question whether you even heard them. A deer getting to its feet makes a distinct thumping sound. Once you hear it, you won't forget it. Pay attention to this sound, as a deer may just be standing there waiting to identify *you*. I've been caught discounting that thumping sound all too often. I'll hear it while I'm walking and pause to listen. Then when I'm listening, I'll talk myself into thinking that I'm hearing things. Then when I take the next step, all I hear is hooves pounding and brush cracking! It all goes back to being patient.

A squirrel rustling or running in the leaves sounds nothing like a deer, but if you hunt where there are turkeys, you know that they *can* sound like a deer. Moose walking can also sound like a deer, except that moose tend to snap more sticks. If I spook a deer by snapping a stick, I'll often give a moose call. Most big-woods bucks are used to living around moose and know the sounds they make. Once you've heard enough deer walking or running in the woods, though, you won't mistake their sound for many other sounds. The one sound that is like no other in the woods is that of a big buck on a mission. It won't be the tiptoeing sound of a doe. A big-woods buck walks with a steady, deliberate, foot-dragging pace, pausing every so often to survey his surroundings. Like the thumping sound of a deer getting to its feet, you'll never forget this sound either.

CHOOSING THE RIGHT ROUTE

Another important element to becoming a good still hunter is being able to choose the right route as you go. You not only have to be able to read the sign and decide where to go, but you also must learn to pick your way through the woods to get there. I've seen many hunters walk into thickets or blowdowns only to have to back out of them and go around. When I started guiding deer hunters, I had the hunter walk in front of me while I pointed out the way to go. But I found that it was too much of a distraction to keep pointing out the way to them, as invariably they would walk toward the worst mess in the woods. Now, I have them follow me. It's important to scan ahead and pick a route. By doing this you can concentrate on looking for deer instead of stumbling over things.

DON'T BE AFRAID TO COVER GROUND

To still-hunt in the big woods, you have to be willing to cover some ground. You may find deer close to a road, but you'll probably find other hunters, too. There is nothing like getting back into the most remote country you can find and going one-on-one with a buck on his home turf. When hunting like this, you never know what kind of buck you might run into. I often walk back in a mile or more and spend the day still-hunting where most hunters don't go. I know that there are areas across the North and West and probably the South where bucks grow up never having contact with human beings. This doesn't mean they are any less wary than bucks that do. On the contrary, I think big bucks have a natural wariness of anything strange to them. That's why they've been able to grow up to be the majestic creatures they are.

Still-hunting is an art. To master it you must be willing to take the time to hone the skills necessary for success. You'll have to leave the ways of the civilized world behind and learn to blend in with nature. You'll have to go wherever your instincts tell you to go without worrying about getting lost. Still-hunting for big-woods bucks is demanding, yet rewarding. Once you master it, hunting any other game animal will become less of a challenge. ∎

These are the ten best bucks I have taken in the last four-teen years. Eight of these deer dressed out over two hundred pounds each. It was an average of three days hunting per buck.

Timing is everything in life especially when related to deer hunting. Catching up with big bucks like this requires skill and a little timing. Knowing when the rut is in full swing will help you set your sights on a trophy like this. This 208-pound buck was shot by Steve Coleman on Thanksgiving Day.

9

ONE WEEK AT A TIME

Bucks in the big woods begin changing their habits as fall approaches. The first big change occurs when the leaves start falling, making visibility better. At this time deer begin moving from their summer areas to their fall areas. The bucks that spent the summer hanging out in a clearcut hidden by the dense new growth now find themselves out in the open. Likewise, the ones that felt safe bedding in the hardwoods, hidden by a carpet of leafy saplings, now find themselves more exposed. This is when most mature bucks will seek out the security of a green bluff or swamp. It's also when bachelor bucks that hung out in groups for the summer go back to their own hideouts.

The next change in deer habits occurs as the rut approaches. In Maine the rifle season starts around November first and runs four weeks, followed by muzzle-loader season. Each week of the season brings changes in bucks' habits, and if you adjust your hunting methods according to what the deer are doing each week, you'll be more successful. Weather is also a big factor in choosing a hunting method, but I'll talk about that in another chapter.

WEEK ONE

During Week One—the first week of November—bucks are in their prerut period. The dominant bucks are saving energy for the upcoming breeding season, when experience has taught them that they will need it. They check on the signposts in their territory to see if any new

This willow brush rub is still green. The buck that did this had not been gone very long.

This is the chance you've been waiting for. If you hesitate, he'll be gone!

bucks are moving in. They also keep the younger bucks that may want to challenge them in their place. They don't travel far in a day, and some days they may not do much more than stretch their legs and feed around a little. Even when there's snow on the ground, a big buck can be hard to locate. Sometimes I've walked all day in the snow and never found a buck track I wanted to follow. For all of these reasons Week One can be the most difficult week to hunt.

There are, however, advantages to hunting this week. If you don't care for cold weather, this early-season week of the hunt tends to be warmer than the later weeks. The bucks haven't been pressured yet, and they're at their maximum weight. There are ways to take advantage of bucks' habits this week. If you're a still-hunter, get into a buck's hideout or hunt around his travel corridors. If you like to hunt the mountains, spend your time high up in the green growth. I like to find places with spruce and fir trees that are tall enough to see under and knobs I can peek over as I hunt along. Usually in these places there are moose trails to walk in, making for quiet going. Be prepared for quick shooting in areas like this, as visibility is usually less than forty yards.

If you hunt the ridges, go where the hardwoods meet the green growth. I like to stay just inside the green—it gives me cover, I can see down into the hardwoods, and it's much quieter walking there than in the hardwood leaves. Bucks often lie on that edge. They feel secure with their back to the thick green growth, and they can watch for danger from below. More than likely they came up from below to bed and are watching their back track.

Another good still-hunting place during Week One is in cedar swamps. It's quiet walking, and there's plenty of cover to hide you and a buck. All of the places I've recommended for Week One are good to hunt any of the weeks, but they're especially good for the first week, as the weather tends to be warmer and the bucks, who already have their winter coats and a good layer of fat, seek out cool places where they can be comfortable. Because buck movement is limited, still-hunting may be more productive than stand-hunting—you go to the deer rather than expect them to come to you.

AN ENERGY-SAVING BUCK

One day during the first week of a hunting season, Sue Morse and I had been still- hunting some hardwood ridges and green bluffs. There was snow on the ground and we were trying to find a good track. We had found some average-size tracks, but nothing we were interested in. It was getting late, and we needed to work our way back to the truck before it got dark. We had made a big circle and were above a cedar swamp that ran along a brook. On the other side of the brook was on old softwood clear-cut that had grown up so thick a rabbit would have had a hard time getting through. Since it was the quickest way back to the truck, we headed into the swamp. I told Sue I had found bucks hanging out here before, but it was almost dark, so we didn't have time to hunt it properly. We had pushed our way into the cedars about a hundred yards when I heard a crack in front of me. I looked just in time to see the back end of a big deer going over a blowdown thirty yards away. Shooting time was over, so there was nothing we could do but go look at the track. As I suspected, it was a monster track. There was no bed where he was standing, so I followed the track back, and thirty yards away was the bed where he had spent the day. This buck's track was nowhere to be found out in the hardwoods—he was apparently spending all of his time holed up in the swamp saving energy for the upcoming rut. :●

If it's warm, deers' daytime activity can be limited during Week One, but a cold snap may trigger them to move about.

FIND THE BED, FIND THE BUCK

One year when I was still lobstering and hunting only when I could find the time, I headed north in the middle of Week One with a couple of friends. When we arrived at camp that night we discovered that it had been warm and there was no snow on the ground. We awoke the next morning to discover that the temperature had dropped to twenty degrees and it was spitting snow. We were planning to hunt a new area that I had scouted a few weeks before the season. It was a long mountain with green bluffs on top and a lot of good hardwood ridges. When we split up in the morning, our plan was for Bruce to take one side of the mountain and Raymond to take the other. I'd hunt the green bluffs on top.

As I worked my way up the mountain in the crunchy leaves, I noticed that the snow pelting the leaves was helping to cover the sound of my footsteps. The higher I got, the more deer tracks I saw punched in the leaves. I came to a saddle in the mountain and found where a buck had been rubbing some trees along an old skid trail. The rubs were fresh—the bright green layer under the bark hadn't faded yet. As I sorted through the tracks in the leaves, I found where the buck had gone up a narrow ravine toward the top of the mountain. As I followed his track I realized that this must be his regular travel route, since he followed a run with all the tracks going in the same direction. The track led to some mossy ledges on top of a bluff. By now there was half an inch of snow, and it was hard to stay on the track. By trial and error I managed to find where he had gone down the other side of the bluff and back into the green growth. As I pushed my way into the thick spruce, I stepped into his bed. I first thought that I had jumped him out, but as I looked closer I discovered there was a dusting of snow in the bed and a walking track leaving. I assumed he had spent the night there and as it got colder he had decided it was comfortable enough to move around.

My excitement rose—now I had snow to track on and a buck just ahead of me. I followed him down the other side of the mountain into a small hardwood bowl. By now the track had only a few flakes in it, so I knew he was close. I kept to the edge of the green growth on the side of the ridge, taking one step at a time and studying the woods ahead. After a few more steps I caught movement under a fir tree fifty yards in front of me. I saw antlers twisting around in the limbs and a leg moving as he made a scrape. Then the movement stopped and I couldn't see a thing. A moment later he appeared, walking broadside right into the open hardwoods. I put the bead on his shoulder and touched off the shot, and he sank to the ground right where he was standing. When I ran down, there lay a perfect ten-pointer with beautiful light-colored antlers.

If you're a stand-hunter, here are some suggestions for stand sites that will increase your odds of success the first week of the season. The best place to stand-hunt during Week One is in the area around a buck's bedroom. This is where he feels most secure, and he spends the majority of his time here during the prerut period. These places are not always easy to find. They are usually in secluded areas with good cover that offers the bucks protection from intruders.

Another good place is along rub lines—especially at signpost rubs. Finding these areas is covered in Chapter 5, "Take a Stand."

WHERE WAS PATIENCE WHEN WE NEEDED IT?

One year during Week One I was still-hunting on bare ground with Sue Morse, and we stumbled across a good stand-hunting site. We were hunting along a small spring brook that ran down from a mountain through the hardwoods. We came across one rub after another, and then we came to a trail cutting across the brook. We began looking around and found about twenty-five rubs within a two-hundred-yard area.. I told Sue there had to be several bucks using this area and I was confident that if we sat here for a day or two she would kill a buck. We set up some scent and decided to come back in as early as we could the next morning to take a stand. We found a good spot to sit where we could look down on the trail and brook. Then we put out some estrous doe scent in canisters and made our way out, looking for the easiest way to return in the morning.

We arrived the next morning in anticipation of seeing a monster buck come wandering through the area. After freshening the scent canisters, we settled in to wait, even if it took all day. The morning had turned cold and the sky was gray as usual. The morning wait was uneventful, and I was beginning to get restless. Since I'm not a sitter, this was bordering on torture for me. At noon I told Sue I had to stretch my legs, take a walk, and do some scouting since we hadn't checked out the area behind us the day before. She said she'd like to go, too. I told her she'd have a better chance at a buck if she stuck it out here, but she was tired of sitting, so we headed off up the ridge. About an hour later it started to snow and snowed for two hours, covering the ground with about an inch of the white stuff.

We didn't see anything that afternoon and didn't return to our sitting spot, but we decided to go back in the following morning and check on the spot. As we got to the trail crossing the brook, we discovered a big buck track half-filled with snow. We came to the same conclusion: this buck had come down the trail during the snow the day before. Nothing else had to be said. We had made our decision to leave the day before, and we had paid the consequences. ☙

WEEK TWO

Week Two is the beginning of the rut period. Although very few does are ready to breed during Week Two, bucks begin actively searching them out. A buck knows

This signpost rub had been used many years ago. It was growing around the old wound and then another buck chose to make it his signpost.

the location of every doe in his range and starts making the rounds hoping to find a receptive one. More buck sign will appear. Bucks actively rub trees, strengthening their necks in case they have to do battle. Scrape lines start to appear in the woods. The bucks are laying down their calling cards for any doe that may be interested.

I believe this is the best week for stand-hunting. One reason is that since the bucks are beginning to move more, you have a good chance of seeing them. This is especially true if you set up along rub and scrape lines. Another reason is that since very few does are in estrus, there's not much of a chance that a buck will be spending time with one instead of making his usual rounds through his territory. If you find the right location and commit to putting in your time, sooner or later Ol' Mossy-Horns will come slipping along. Almost every hunter I've guided who committed himself to staying on a stand all week (if that's what it took) has seen or killed a buck. The key is *commitment*.

Still-hunting will also be better this week than during Week One. Instead of having to crawl through the green growth to try and find a bedded buck, you'll be more likely to catch a buck out and about. I like to focus my still-hunting this week in the same areas that are good for stand-hunting. By quietly sneaking along a rub or scrape line, taking the time to look and listen often, you may catch that old buck looking around. Since the bucks are traveling more, they are laying down more tracks. So even if there's no snow and leaves to cover the trails, you'll begin to see tracks punched into the leaves, making it easier to find your way from one rub or scrape to another.

CLOSE CALL

One day while still-hunting around some swale bogs, I came to the edge of an old chopping. As I worked my way up the edge of it, I came to where a buck had thrashed a scrub willow. It was still bright green, so I knew he'd been there recently. A good track was punched into the frozen leaves heading toward a patch of green growth. I had just started down the track when I heard a crack and then saw a deer running up ahead. I had no chance for a shot and waited for him to settle down. I followed the track to where he had run from and discovered a fresh scrape with a running track leaving it. If I had been a few minutes earlier I might have snuck up on him and caught him making the rub. But this time the two points didn't connect.

Often by Week Two the north country will have snow. Usually it's a wet snow that hangs on every tree limb, limiting visibility. This is great tracking weather—the damp snow quiets the leaves, making it easy to walk silently. The snow in the tree limbs also helps to muffle noises you make going through the brush.

TRACKING IN THE SNOW

I was tracking a buck I had just jumped one year in this kind of weather. He wasn't particularly nervous and was staying just ahead of me. I followed him out of the green growth, across a hardwood opening, and into more green growth. He moved slowly and started to feed, so I took my time. The snow was so heavy in the fir limbs that I could see barely thirty feet. I came to a snow-laden fir and was looking around trying to see where the track led. All of a sudden I caught a flash of brown between two trees. I waited a minute and then moved ahead to discover that the buck had been standing ten feet from me on the other side of the fir. I never did get that buck, since he stayed in the thick firs and never gave me another chance to approach him.

WEEK THREE

This is the week the rut starts to swing into high gear. More does are coming into estrus and leaving that special scent in the air that the bucks are looking for. A buck now travels day and night until he finds a receptive doe. Then he stays with her for a couple of days, making sure he passes along his genes for future generations. If a buck finds a doe he thinks is ready to breed, he pokes and prods her until she submits. If she's not ready, she'll run from him, and this is when the chasing begins. He'll follow her every move like a lost puppy dog, paying little attention to anything else. This is the time to catch him off guard. I once watched an average-size buck chase a doe

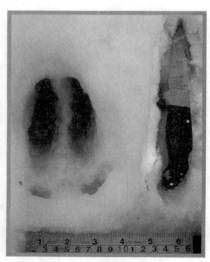

If you see a track such as this you'll want to take up the chase. You can tell it's a mature buck by the three-inch width and the dew claws wider than the hoof. (Courtesy: Susan C. Morse)

85

all around a hardwood bowl. She'd race for the ridge on one side of the bowl with the buck right behind. When she stopped he'd try to mount her, and she'd race for the other side. I watched this show for five minutes before they finally disappeared into the thick brush.

If you're going to take a stand this week, you may want to switch tactics. Although scrape lines are still a good bet, the drawback to hunting them is that if a buck is with a doe, he may not use the trail for quite some time. I have seen active scrape lines not be visited for a week, which could be pretty discouraging if you were sitting there waiting. A better bet is to set up around an area where there's plenty of doe sign. Look for feeding sign such as ground where they've pawed for fern buds or places where they've browsed on twigs. You'll also find beds nearby, as does tend to lie down close to their feeding areas. By setting up in such a place you increase your chances of seeing a buck, since every one in the area will know where the does are and check on them routinely.

Still-hunting around these same areas will also be more effective during Week Three.

STILL-HUNTING DOE AREAS

I sent a hunter around one side of a big green bluff where I knew a bunch of does were hanging out. When we met later that day he told me about a buck he'd seen. He had still-hunted the hardwoods along the base of the bluff until lunchtime, and in the afternoon he had retraced his steps. About halfway back, he heard the distinct sound of a deer running up ahead. It was too far away to see, so he started to run toward

When you see a doe, don't move. There may be a buck nearby.

the sound. When he stopped to listen again, he saw a doe running about a hundred yards ahead of him. He thought a buck might be chasing her, so he ran again, trying to close the gap. When he stopped again, he saw another doe running from the bluff with a monster buck on her tail. As the buck sailed over a blown-down log, he saw a huge set of golden antlers. The buck stopped for a moment, but was out of sight behind some brush. Then he took off again and my hunter had no chance for a shot. He said seeing a buck like that made the whole hunt.

A doe can be a great decoy this week, so be patient if you see one. Watch what she does and how she acts, since there may be a buck around that you don't see. If she flicks her tail and keeps looking behind her or in the same direction repeatedly, chances are a buck is there or one has been following her.

When tracking during Week Two, you never know what might happen. You could follow a buck on a mission to find a doe and he could go for miles without stopping. When you get on one of these bucks you'll have to switch into high gear if you expect to catch up to him. I tracked a buck like this once from daylight until dark and got only one quick look at him. He never lay down in all that time and kept going the same direction. By the time he crossed a logging road late in the afternoon there were two mountains and about six miles between me and my truck. That buck had somewhere to go and wasn't wasting any time getting there.

On the other hand, you may get on the trail of a buck that finds a doe or is already with a doe and they may not be far away. When you're tracking one of these bucks, pay attention to what the doe does—she's the one keeping an eye out for danger. If her fawns are with her it's even more difficult to get close since there are more sets of eyes and ears to detect you. Many times I've had a doe spook before I could get a shot at the buck she was with.

WEEK FOUR

The rut is still in high gear this week. Bucks are searching out does day and night, and chasing is still evident in the woods. Use the same tactics you used for Week Three. It's rare when there's no snow for tracking this week, and some years there's enough to start the deer moving toward their winter yards. In these areas a good canopy of softwood keeps the snow from getting too deep and limiting the deers' ability to move about and find food. This cover also protects them from the harsh wind and brutal cold of a northern winter, when temperatures can get down to forty degrees below zero. It can get extremely cold this week, as the days are almost at their shortest length of the year.

Although there's still lots of activity, the bucks are starting to get tired after a week of steady doe chasing and may try to catch a few hours' rest between their travels. Sometimes a buck may actually close his eyes and even stretch out on the ground and look as if he were lying there dead, so if you pay close attention when tracking, you may just kill a buck before he can get up out of his bed. Mike, my remote camp guide, killed a buck that way one year. He had tracked the buck up through some softwood bluffs. Then the buck went out into the hardwoods and turned uphill. As Mike eased his way along, he looked ahead and saw this nice eight-point buck lying down staring in one direction, and he never saw Mike approach. He must have been asleep, since Mike was within twenty yards of him in the open hardwoods. Finding a buck this tired can be your big chance— even if you spook him, he's not inclined to move very fast or very far.

Deer love to eat the bark of elderberry bush, especially after the snow has covered the ground. (Courtesy: Susan C. Morse)

A TIRED BUCK ELUDES A HUNTER

One year my fourth-week hunter and I picked up a smoking fresh buck track in the morning. We followed it through a swale bog and into a fir thicket. As we made our way into the thicket, we came to the buck's bed, which was barely packed in the snow, indicating that he had been lying there for only a few minutes before he ran out the other side of the thicket and back across the bog. Then he went up a ridge and lay down in his track. He saw us coming and ran again, only to bed down again within five hundred yards. Now I knew this buck was worn out; he wanted nothing but rest, and we were an annoyance. Once we figured out his routine, we'd get a chance at him. We kept pushing along, hoping to catch him lying down, but he always kept the advantage. Finally he headed back to where he had started from and we ran to head him off. We got to an opening just in time to see him walking through the other side about a hundred yards away. The hunter fired two shots as the buck disappeared into the firs, but apparently there were just too many branches to allow the bullet to hit its mark, and he didn't connect. We saw that buck once more before darkness fell, and then we made our way out of the woods.

During Week Four, the chances of a buck being with a doe are still good, and you may have a chance to catch a buck whose attention is focused on a doe. I found a buck like this one year on the last day of rifle season. My hunter that week had killed a buck earlier and had gone home for Thanksgiving. This had been a hard fall for me, as my grandfather had passed away in September and at the same time I had learned that my dad had cancer. The two days before the hunt I had been visiting my dad in the hospital and I needed to get into the woods and try to clear my mind.

A NEW EXPERIENCE

I picked up a good track heading high up on a mountain. I followed the buck through the typical spruce thickets on top and then down the other side, where he found a doe and joined her. As they made their way down some old skid trails, they zigzagged and fed as they went. I knew I'd find them somewhere around the spruce knobs, so I took my time, knowing they didn't suspect that anything was following them. Just as I got to the edge of a ravine, I heard a low grunting noise. At first I thought it was a tree creaking, as the wind was blowing fairly steadily. When I heard it again, I knew it wasn't a tree, and I looked down and saw deer moving below me. The buck followed the doe into some thick brush fifty yards away. He looked big, as his track had indicated, but I couldn't see his antlers, so I held off on shooting. Since I knew I might have to wait a while before I could get a better look, I sat down. As I watched them, the buck mounted the doe and began to breed her. My hunt was made right then, as this was the first time I had seen breeding in the wild. When they finished, the doe walked across the skid trail I was sitting in and began to feed against a ledge. I knew sooner or later the buck would join her. I didn't have to wait long before he stepped into the trail and stopped. He was a huge-bodied buck well over two hundred pounds, and when he looked in my direction I could see why I hadn't seen much for horns. His left beam was broken off at the brow point. I decided to let him go for another year. I didn't need the meat and didn't want a half-rack mount, so why kill him just to say I had? I guess I felt in some small way that letting that buck live might make up for the my dad's life that was soon to end. Two weeks later Dad passed on. ☙

MUZZLE-LOADER WEEK

In Maine muzzle-loader week is the week following Thanksgiving or the first week in December. In other areas there might be a shotgun season this week. In most areas this is probably the time when the deer have the least amount of hunting pressure. Most hunters have given up by now or don't like the cold. This is also the

This is the bed of a truly monstrous buck– probably near the three-hundred-pound mark.

beginning of the postrut period. Most does have been bred by now, and bucks begin to turn their attention toward survival. They have lost as much as thirty percent of their body weight during the rut and need to put some fat back on in order to make it through the winter. They spend more time feeding and resting. It's likely that there's enough snow and cold to start them moving to their winter yards. If this happens, you may have the chance to see more deer this week than at any other time as they concentrate into smaller areas.

Stand-hunting can be very productive during muzzle-loading season. Find a migration trail that leads to the yard and set up there. These trails will be easy to pick out in the snow because of the unusual amount of tracks all going in one direction. One of my hunters sat on one of these trails and saw twenty-three does in one day, and then a buck finally came along to shoot.

Still-hunting slowly along the trails in the yard is a great way to hunt this week. By moving slowly and looking constantly, you should be able to run into a buck. It's important to remember that you are where the deer are, and covering a lot of ground is not your objective. Spending all day in a very small area can be productive, as deer will be moving about on these trails and new deer will be arriving every day.

Tracking is very difficult in a yard—there are too many tracks to sort through and you'll spend most of your time looking at the ground instead of in the woods. This is, nonetheless, my favorite

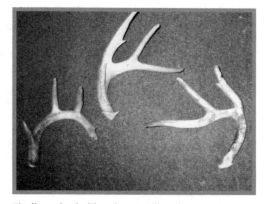

Finding sheds like these will tell you where a buck is staying during the winter. This will really help out your late season hunting if the snow gets deep.

time to track, but I don't spend my time in a yard. Instead I try to pick up a track back on a ridge somewhere. The big old bucks are usually the last to get to the yard, and they may not yard at all. Some bucks prefer to spend the winter alone on a secluded green bluff, where they feel safe from the coyotes that follow the other deer into the yard (see Chapter 2, "The Nomadic Whitetail").

KEEP YOUR POWDER DRY!

As I said, the bucks in the yard spend a lot of time feeding, and they usually don't travel far. One year I cut a big buck's track where he had crossed an unused logging road. I check this spot every year, as it's a regular buck crossing in a saddle between two long mountain ridges. He dropped down into a ravine and came to an old skid trail lined with small cedars. He had fed heavily on the cedars, and as I looked around I discovered that another good buck had also been there. I sorted through the track and discovered that the two bucks had gone off together. Little did I know that I had already spooked them— they were lying only seventy-five yards from where I was. I gave them half an hour to settle down before taking up the tracks again.

They stayed together as they worked their way through a cedar bog and out into an old chopping. A smaller buck joined them, and all three wandered through the chopping. The small buck left as the two big ones entered an area of uncut spruce knolls. By now I knew I was getting close, and I was taking one step at a time when a buck jumped through an opening in the firs ahead of me. I had no time for a shot as he disappeared behind a blowdown. I grunted a couple of times and waited a few minutes. I eased along the track again as he started to walk through thick firs that were head-high and heavy with snow, making the visibility about ten feet. As I broke out into an opening on a knoll, there he stood, only thirty yards away. I counted five points with a thick main beam on the side facing me. I aimed at his shoulder, squeezed the trigger, and my gun went *click!* I couldn't believe it! The buck never moved. I thought there might be ice in the bolt so it didn't strike the cap hard enough. I cocked the bolt again and pulled the trigger, only to hear the same click. I dropped to one knee to put on another cap just as the buck walked into the firs again.

With a new cap on, I walked down to where he stood. As I was trying to decided what to do next, the other buck walked out of the firs twenty yards from me. This buck was bigger bodied and had eight points, but before I could pull up my gun he disappeared again. I could see that he was heading toward another opening, so I stayed where I

My first muzzle-loader buck: a high-racked seven-pointer, that I tracked while he was with a doe.

was. Just as he stepped into the opening, I squeezed the trigger again. This time the cap went *snap,* but the gun still didn't go off. All I could do was watch him walk over the hill. I tried to decide whether I should wrap the gun around a tree or just make a fire and burn it. It took me a few minutes to calm down after those two monster bucks got away, and I decided I had to keep the gun if I was going to get one of them. I took it apart and recharged it with fresh powder before taking up the tracks again. I never got another chance at those bucks, but I did learn a hard lesson about keeping my powder dry. At dark I ended up right where I had started in the morning; those bucks had not traveled in more than a half-mile area.

The next year on the first morning of muzzle-loader season, I headed for the same crossing. As I had hoped, a good buck track headed down into the ravine in the same place as the one had the year before. I followed him down the ravine, where he found a doe and followed her into the cedar bog. I thought he might be one of the bucks that had escaped me the year before. When they got into the bog they started feeding, so I knew they were close. I took one step at a time, searching every inch of the surrounding woods. It took me about an hour to cover a hundred yards, but I knew I had to be patient. By now it had started to snow, with heavy, wet flakes making the visibility in the bog very poor. As I was ducking under a snow-laden cedar, I spotted the outline of a deer's back. On the other side of a tree I could see his head and the base of his antlers, confirming that it was the buck. I aimed behind his shoulder, squeezed the trigger, and this time there was a *boom* and the smoke hung in the air as he crashed off through the bog. This time I had taken precautions to make sure my powder and caps were dry. I kept everything in resealable plastic bags and put duct tape over the end of my barrel and over the bolt. I had reloaded and started toward where the buck had been when I saw another deer take off. It was the doe—she had been standing only thirty feet from me the whole time.

When I got to where the buck had stood, I could see blood sprayed on the snow all along the track, and he was lying dead thirty yards away. As soon as I saw him I knew he wasn't one of the bucks from the year before. This buck was a seven-pointer that didn't have as much mass as the other two, but since he was my first muzzle-loader buck, he was special to me.

Contrary to popular belief, deer, especially mature bucks, often move more during inclement weather. This includes snow, rain, and heavy winds. Savvy deer hunters are sure to be found stalking through the big-woods during and after snow falls. (Courtesy: Roman Jaskolski)

10

WEATHER OR NOT

Weather is probably the factor that most affects the actions and movement of deer and all of the other animals in the woods. Some say the rut is more important, but I've seen deer go mostly nocturnal when the weather has turned unseasonably warm. Since they live out in the elements, it makes sense that their safety and comfort directly correlate with what the weather is doing. By understanding what effects the ever-changing weather conditions have on deer, you'll be in a better position to take advantage of them. Since you can't change the weather, learn to adapt your hunting techniques to it. There are so many variables in weather—from warm and rainy to cold and snowy, and everything in between—that there's no cut-and-dried rule for each condition.

WARM WEATHER

Warm weather, especially in the north country, is toughest to hunt in. Deer already have their winter coats and a heavy layer of fat from the summer's good feed, and they're just not comfortable moving around much. Whether you're still-hunting or stand-hunting, the obvious places to hunt when it's warm are cool, shady ones. Look for swamps and bogs or hunt along streams and rivers. Bucks love these areas in any weather, as they provide good cover.

Another good bet is in green growth at the tops of ridges or mountains—you'll find cool, wet areas in these places too, and often a breeze will be blowing across the ridges, making it seem even cooler. You'll know if you're in the right area because you'll feel the temperature change. In warm weather I like to still-hunt these areas. I don't waste much time out in the hardwoods. I move quickly through them so I can spend most of my time in the more productive areas.

COLD WEATHER

Cold weather gets deer moving. They are more comfortable moving around when it's cold, and they also need to feed more to stay warm and maintain their fat reserve for winter, when they won't be able to get as much feed. When it's extremely cold— when the mercury dips below zero—they stay bedded at night and move about during the day as it warms. If you can tough out the cold weather, it's a great time to see deer. It was a zero-degree day in the story titled "Number 11" (Chapter 13) when I saw eleven deer by one o'clock, all moving about.

If it's cold and sunny, a big old buck may stretch out on top of a hardwood ridge where he can watch everything below. If there's wind with the cold, deer will usually bed on the leeward side of a ridge, where they have shelter from the wind, and they'll also seek shelter in the softwoods, where the spruce and fir limbs stop the wind.

The increase in deer activity makes cold weather a great time to take a stand, but be sure to wear proper clothing. It's also good for still-hunting, as you have a better chance of seeing a buck moving about instead of having to find one bedded. If there's snow on the ground, it goes without saying that it's going to be a great time to track a buck.

RAINY WEATHER

It's amazing how rain can change hunting conditions. It can cool the temperature and increase deer movement. Rain also dampens the leaves, making it easier to hear something besides your own footsteps as you walk. Other than when it's snowing, rainy weather is my favorite time to hunt. Rain makes the day gray and minimizes shadows, so it's easier to see into every corner of the woods. Deer activity is good unless it's a hard, wind-driven rain, when there won't be much activity by any of the animals in the woods.

HUNTING IN DRIVING RAIN

On one such day I was lucky enough to experience an exception to that rule. When I left camp that morning the temperature was a balmy forty-five degrees with fog hanging in the mountains. As I hunted my way up a mountain, thunder started to rumble in the distance. Soon I was right in the middle of a thunder-and-lightning storm, with lightning cracking all around me. I hunkered down until it passed, and then it started to rain so hard I was wet through to the skin in five minutes. It rained off and on for the next couple of hours as I continued hunting my way toward the top of the mountain.

By the time I had reached the top, the wind had come up and the temperature was dropping fast. All I had on was a wool shirt over my long-john top, and I knew I couldn't hunt all day wet and cold, so I decided to hunt my way back to camp and get a dry shirt and jacket. Since I had come up one hardwood ravine to the top, I went back down a different one. I had just started through the other ravine when I spotted a deer standing like a statue in the hardwoods below me. I couldn't see antlers, as his head was behind a tree, but I could see that the body was big, so I waited. Finally he turned his head, I saw his rack, and that was all I needed to see before touching off the -06. As I walked down to where he lay, I was a little disappointed by the size of his antlers and thought he'd never hit two hundred pounds. I changed my mind by the time I had dragged him back to camp, and he ended up tipping the scales at 215 pounds.

This proves that no matter what the conditions are, there's always a chance to kill a big buck.

Probably the best kind of weather for finding active deer is the calm right after the end of a hard, wind-driven rain. It's a magical time when everything in the woods seems to come alive. If you've ever experienced it, you know what I mean. The birds chirp and the squirrels chatter. It seems as if by command all the deer start to move. You'll want to be in the woods when this happens.

THE CALM AFTER THE STORM, PART ONE

Once back when we were hunting out of a camper up north, a wind and rain storm started in the evening. The camper rocked all night as the rain pelted the sides of it. I had told Deb I was going to take her out the next day, but at daylight the rain was still pounding, so we decided to catch a little more sleep. The next time I woke up, the rain had stopped and it was quiet outside. I woke Deb and told her we had to eat quickly and get into the woods. After a quick breakfast, Dad drove us to the end of a long ridge. The plan was that we'd hunt our way across it and Dad would pick us up at the other end when it turned dark. It was about a mile to the top of the ridge, and there was a skid road we could walk on most of the way.

My thunderstorm buck. I took this 215-pound seven-pointer still-hunting when it was raining so hard it made the woods appear to be in a fog.

We took our time, still-hunting our way up and stopping often to look around. I had gotten a little ahead of Deb, and as I was waiting for her to catch up, I spotted a nice buck feeding along about fifty yards in front of me. His head was down, so I motioned for her to hurry. I kept an eye on him as she worked her way up, motioning for her to stop when he lifted his head. By the time she got to me the buck was only thirty yards away and standing broadside with his head behind a tree. As she pulled up her gun, all I could think of was that she was about to shoot her first buck. But when she squeezed the trigger, her gun went *click,* and the buck's ears tipped forward, searching for the source of the sound. I could hear her fumbling with her semi-auto, and when I looked over I saw that she had double-fed a bullet as she tried to chamber a new round. When I looked back at the buck I could see by his ears that he was about to make his exit. I drew my rifle up, and when the bead was on his shoulder, I fired. He went into the air, and as he cleared the skid road I fired again. We watched him crash through the brush and fall about forty yards away. Needless to say, Deb was pretty upset, and to this day she tells people about how *I* shot *her* buck. :➔

THE CALM AFTER THE STORM, PART TWO

One night in remote camp we had the same kind of weather. This time it was after an unseasonably warm day—a high of sixty-five degrees. When I awoke before daylight it was still raining, but the temperature had dropped to forty degrees. I woke my hunter, Ed, and asked him if

Ed's 190-pound seven-pointer, taken after a night of howling wind and rain.

he wanted to go out and get wet or wait a little to see what happened. He said he'd wait, so my guide Mike and I went over to the cook tent to get the coffee going. Mike and I agreed that as soon as the rain stopped the deer would come out of the woodwork. In about an hour the rain quit, and then I noticed a familiar noise—snow sifting onto the tent roof. I looked out to confirm it and checked the thermometer again. It was down to thirty-two degrees.

I ran over to wake Ed up and tell him the good news. He got dressed as Mike and I cooked breakfast. It was Thanksgiving week. Mike didn't have any hunters and had killed his big buck the day before. During breakfast we discussed our plan for the day. We decided to still-hunt some softwood choppings around a pond where I knew a good bunch of does gathered. We drove down near the head of the pond and went into the woods there. It was still spitting snow, and the wind was switching back and forth.

Ed and I had gone only about a hundred fifty yards when a buck jumped out from behind a blowdown thirty yards from us. As he bounced down a skid trail I saw that he had only one antler. I pointed him out to Ed and told him to hold off, as that was not what we were after. The buck turned into the spruces and headed toward the pond. I told Ed we were going to ease along grunting and see if we could get a better look at his body size. I grunted as we moved through some thick firs. After about fifty yards we came to an opening. I looked toward where the buck had gone and didn't see anything. Then I looked the other way and there was a deer standing in a skid trail twenty-five yards from us. Its head was down, so I figured it was a doe feeding. As I pointed it out to Ed, its head came up and we could see a set of antlers. Ed pulled his gun up and fired. The buck took two jumps and stopped. Ed fired again and the buck bolted into the firs and dropped. We had been in the woods only fifteen minutes and had already seen two bucks! This is why the period after a rain is one of my favorite times to be in pursuit of a big-woods buck.

WINDY WEATHER

Wind is extremely variable. There are light breezes and there are gale winds. There are fair-weather winds and foul-weather winds. All of them affect deer differently. Since wind is a common phenomenon to deer, most of it has very little effect on their activity. The exception is a strong, blustery wind, especially when it is associated with rain or snow. This kind of wind definitely subdues deer activity. High wind greatly decreases the information deer receive from their noses, ears, and eyes. Odors their noses might detect are blown about the woods in the gusts. As the wind blows through the trees and rattles the leaves, they can hear nothing but nearby sounds. The movement of trees and leaves makes it difficult for deer to distinguish between them and something or someone dangerous. Strong wind makes deer spooky and puts them on high alert. They're difficult to approach and usually run at the slightest hint of danger.

WIND + SNOW = GREAT HUNTING

I watched a buck acting this way while hunting opening day. Maine residents can hunt the Saturday before opening day, and I always do, since I don't get much time to hunt while I'm guiding. This particular year we were blessed with a snowstorm that started Friday night and continued through the day on Saturday. There was a strong wind, making blizzard-like conditions in the mountains. I knew there wouldn't be much activity, so my plan was to still-hunt the green bluffs on a mountain in hopes of catching a buck bedded down. I spooked several does before I reached the top of the ridge. Then I hunted along the ridge until I came to a saddle that cut the mountain in half. I knew the terrain was open down in the saddle, so I moved slowly along the edge hoping to spot a buck lying out of the wind. When I didn't see anything I dropped down into the saddle and found a big fresh bed with a track running from it. At first I thought I had spooked him, but I knew there was no way I could have missed seeing him leave. After taking up the track I confirmed that I hadn't spooked him—he had never stopped to look back on his track. He had run down off the mountain to lie in a softwood bog where there was more shelter from the storm. I jumped him there and he headed across the side of the mountain. I spooked him again—out of an old chopping—and then he headed back across the mountain. He finally headed toward the same saddle where he had been earlier.

As I followed his track along a finger ridge in the open hardwoods, I kept my eye on the ravine below. The wind was swirling and the snow blowing, making visibility poor, but something caught my attention. As I scanned through the snow, I could make out the shape of a deer lying under a big spruce tree at about a hundred yards. I was kicking myself now for not bringing my binoculars. I finally made out the head and could see horns, but couldn't tell how big they were as the spruce limbs were hanging down covering most of his head. I could tell he was nervous by the way he snapped his head back and forth, looking on his back track and then to the sides. I knew this must be the buck I had been tracking and had him figured for about two hundred pounds, so I wanted to see what he had for horns before deciding whether or not to shoot.

I put a big hardwood tree between us and closed the distance to sixty yards, but I still couldn't get a good look at his antlers. He was still acting nervous as the wind cracked tree limbs and they dropped to the ground. I was thinking of a way to make him stand up when suddenly he did. Now his rack was completely hidden, but I knew he'd have to come into the open hardwoods if he wanted to go anywhere. He turned and started to walk, so I stepped out from behind the tree with my gun up. When he stepped into view I could see by his profile that he was an eight-pointer with a high rack, but he didn't move ahead. He was a nice-looking buck with a dark coat and was around the two hundred pound mark as I had figured. I decided to let him go. I brought my gun down just as he turned and started to bound away. When he did I saw that he had a wide rack, well outside his ears. If I had seen that spread before, I might not have passed him up. That buck never knew I was there, and I was grateful to be able to watch him. When I was younger I didn't like to hunt in the wind as I was discouraged about not being able to hear anything. I also didn't like the fact that I everything was moving, making it harder for me to see the deer. I finally realized that because the deer couldn't see me either, the playing field was level. When it's windy, you truly are one-on-one with a buck. Even if leaves are crunching underfoot, the sound barely travels. It becomes a game of who can spot whom first.

WIND GIVES ME A CHANCE AT A GREAT BUCK

Another year on opening day, the ground was bare and the wind was blowing at a pretty good clip. I didn't think there would be much moving, so I figured I'd cover some ground and do some scouting. I decided to try a mountain I hadn't hunted before. My plan for the day was to hunt my way around the whole mountain, looking for scrape lines and signpost rub areas.

By early afternoon I'd gone about three quarters of the way around and had found a lot of good buck sign. The sun was bright, creating glare, and with the wind keeping everything moving, it was hard to see. I was following some tracks punched in the leaves down an old survey line spotted with yellow paint. I stopped at the edge of a new chopping. I'd been standing there for a few minutes looking around when I caught movement out in the chopping. I saw a big-bodied buck step through an opening about fifty yards away. A few minutes later I saw an antler and an eye. The buck stood there for a few minutes and then turned and stepped through another opening, and I had no chance for a shot. As he disappeared, it looked as though he was starting to lie down. I waited a little longer and didn't see him, so I tried sneaking toward him. For a while I used a yellow birch top the woodcutters had left as cover. I started inching ahead, taking a step each time the wind gusted. After I'd gone about ten yards, a doe came walking above me at twenty yards. I let her get out of sight before moving again. I moved another ten yards and spotted another doe feeding below me at forty yards. Now I knew I was going to have to be really careful—there were does on both sides of me and a buck somewhere in front of me. I eased ahead slowly, using the wind for cover, all the time searching ahead for the buck. I was close to where I thought the buck might have lain down, but I couldn't see him.

As I waited for the wind to gust, I looked down at the doe, and when I looked back ahead, there stood the buck not twenty yards off, facing away. He had been bedded in a little hollow and had just stood up. When he swung his head around I could see that he had a neck like a Holstein cow and a thick, high, eight-point rack. I knew I was going to have to do something quickly before the wind swirled and he caught my scent. Since his back was toward me, all I could see was his hind end. His front end was in the hollow, so I had no shot at his neck. He was behind a blow-down, and the only shot I had was at the base of his tail. I knew a bullet there would break his back. Back then I was carrying a scoped rifle on fair-weather days, so I put the cross hairs just over the top of the blowdown and fired. He took two jumps and stopped behind another birch top where I couldn't shoot. Then he saw the doe running below and high-tailed in behind her, and they disappeared down over the ridge. I stood there dumbfounded, wondering how I could have missed him. I walked down to where he had stood, and then I could see what had happened. I had shot right into the top of the blowdown. I should have aimed a little higher to compensate for the two inches the scope sits above the bore of the rifle. A big mistake, but there's always something to learn.

Without the wind that day, I'd never have gotten anywhere near that buck. By moving with the wind and using it to cover my movement and sound, I got to within twenty yards of where he was bedded. It *did* take me over half an hour to cover the thirty yards, but it was well worth the time just to get a close look at a buck like that.

SNOWY WEATHER

Snow affects deer differently depending on the time of year and the type of snow. Often the first snow of the year will keep them holed up for a day, and I've seen the first snow come to the north country as early as the beginning of October. I think sensing the oncoming winter makes them nervous. Deer may get up and feed around, but they usually don't travel far. This seems to be especially true of the big bucks. Many times I've roamed all day on the first snow and never found a decent track.

FIRST SNOW MEANS NO DEER SIGHTINGS

One year we didn't have our first snow until the third week of hunting season. It snowed most of the night and then changed to rain before ending. I thought the deer would be moving, as the rut was kicking in. I took a hunter and walked until late afternoon and never cut so much as a doe track. I sent my hunter back to camp the short way while I made another loop on a logging road to check for tracks. Just before dark I found a spot where a buck and two does had crossed the road recently. I followed the track about three hundred yards before seeing them on a hardwood knoll. I backed off, thinking they might stay there overnight and we'd get a chance at the buck in the morning.

Once they get through that first day on the new snow, the deer get back to their normal routines, and their movements from then on are controlled by wind and the other snowstorms that follow. Wind-driven snow has the same effect on deer as wind-driven rain and, as with hunting after a rainstorm, right after a snowstorm is one of the best times to be in the woods. If you're a tracker, you'll be able to tell how old a track is by looking at how much snow is in it and taking note of when the storm ended. Sometimes a buck starts to travel at the end of a storm, and his track may have some snow in it. This doesn't matter—as you follow the track, sooner or later it will be free of snow.

Hunting during a snowstorm is exciting. When you find a track, you'll be able to tell its age within minutes, and your chances of catching a buck looking around greatly increase. When I'm tracking a buck during a snowstorm and I come to the point where there's no snow in the track, I put the brakes on and start scanning every inch of the woods around me, because I know the buck is probably within a hundred yards of me and I want to see him before he sees me. This is a game of hide-and-seek, and I set my pace according to the pace of the buck and the visibility in the woods. Many times I've caught a buck looking when doing this. Sometimes I've connected with good bucks and other times I've let them walk away.

When the snow gets to a certain depth, the deer move toward their yarding areas. If this happens during the rut, you may have to change your hunting area and move with the deer. Fortunately this happens infrequently.

By watching the weather and hunting accordingly you can tremendously increase your chances of taking a big-woods buck. So don't let the weather keep you in camp—you have to be out there in the game if you want to score. ■

Understanding and interpreting signs left by bucks will make any tracker's or stalker's hunt end more successfully. (Courtesy: Ted Rose)

TRACK HIM DOWN

Nothing quite compares to the satisfaction of tracking down and shooting a big buck on a blanket of fresh snow. Taking on this king of the forest on his own turf—and winning—is a worthy accomplishment. Big-woods white-tailed bucks have developed keen instincts to avoid danger from predators. Unlike herd animals that rely on many eyes and ears to alert them to danger, a big-woods buck is on his own. His very existence depends on his ability to avoid or escape from predators, including humans. If a white-tailed buck survives to his fourth year, he's one of the toughest animals on earth to hunt. He constantly watches for danger and rarely lies down where he can't see his back track. We've all heard a story or two about the hunter who followed a track a few hundred yards and found a monster buck standing there waiting to be shot. That's got to be the purest form of dumb luck! I'm not begrudging anyone who's ever shot a buck that way, because I'd do the same if I had the chance, and I'd count my blessings. I figure any buck standing around waiting to be shot needs to be removed from the gene pool.

Of the hundreds of deer I've tracked over the years, though, I've never been lucky enough to find a monster buck that stood still and let me walk up to him, so I've had to develop the skills necessary to help me get close to bucks and create my own luck. The good news is that anybody with patience and persistence can develop these skills, too.

Tracking is not simply the ability to follow in a buck's footsteps. To become consistently successful at tracking you have to develop certain skills: identifying and aging tracks in any weather condition, having a sixth sense to help you become more in tune with your surroundings, being able to move about the woods as if you are a part of them, and knowing the habits of bucks—the when and why of what they do. In essence, you must start to think like bucks do so you can anticipate their moves. Each buck is an individual that has developed his own habits from his life's experiences, but bucks also have habits in common that are part of their genetic makeup. By learning these, you'll have a better chance of anticipating a buck's next move and be on your way to consistently bagging big-woods bucks.

There's something about being in the big woods on the track of a buck in the snow that makes me feel as if I'm in a new realm of hunting that disconnects me from the rest of the world. I can't explain it, and if you've never done it you won't understand it, but once you *do* experience that feeling, you'll be hooked. When I get on a track, I forget about everything and concentrate on nothing else but how I can catch this buck. I guess you could call it living for the moment.

Tracking bucks is the fastest way to learn their habits. When you follow a buck, he'll take you to his hidden haunts—places you might never expect a buck to go. He'll show you where his signposts are and where the does are. Once you've followed enough bucks, you'll start to see the pieces of the puzzle come together. I hope my experiences will help you sort through that puzzle on your way to becoming a big-buck tracker.

READING TRACKS

The first step to becoming a tracker is learning to identify tracks. I've read in books and articles that you can't tell the difference between a buck track and a doe track, but I believe this is false. If you look at the whole picture—and not just at an individual print—you'll be able to tell a buck track from a doe track most of the time. The more experience you have, the better you'll be at distinguishing one from the other. First, look at the print itself.

This is the largest buck track I've ever found. This is a walking print and he is so heavy his toes splay out. (The Leatherman tool pictured at the right is eight inches long.)

HOW BIG IS THE TRACK?

Size is the first thing to consider. There isn't a doe alive that has a track a big as a hog buck's, but it can be difficult to tell a doe track from the track of a medium-sized buck.

ARE ANY DEWCLAWS SHOWING?

If there is less than two inches of snow, a walking doe usually doesn't leave dewclaw prints, but a good buck always leaves them in any amount of snow and even on bare ground. The heavier a buck is, the deeper the prints will be and the more they'll be set back from the hooves. If they're running or there's

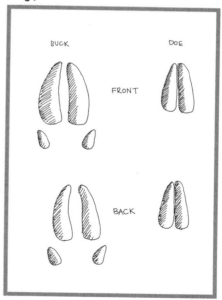

Buck versus Doe Tracks

more snow, both does and bucks leave dewclaw prints, but bucks' dewclaws are larger compared to the size of their hooves than does' are. Bucks' dewclaws also leave a print as wide as or wider than the print of the hoof itself.

Are You Looking at a Front Hoof or a Back Hoof?

There's a big difference. When a deer walks, its back foot steps in the same spot as its front foot, covering the front track; therefore, the print you see will be that of the back foot. This is important to know, since the back foot is smaller than the front. If I find a track that looks good but I'm not sure if I'm going to take it, I follow it until the buck stops to look around or make a scrape. There he will leave a front hoofprint that I can size up so I can decide whether to keep tracking him. Once you're sure you have a buck track by sizing up the prints, you'll learn more about the buck's size as you start to follow him.

How Are the Prints Placed?

Measure the distance between the left print and the right. If it's eight inches or more, it's a good buck—and if it's more than twelve inches, it's a monster. This distance develops as a buck gets older and his chest gets deeper. Notice whether his hooves are dragging, especially when there is very little snow. The older a buck is, the more he will tend to drag his feet.

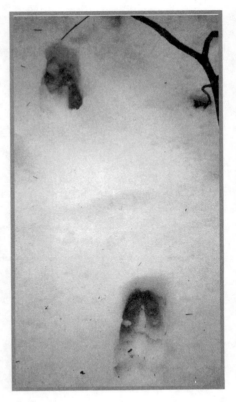

This shows the back foot stepping directly on top of the front foot.

This buck went around the two-foot opening between the trees. This indicates that he is carrying a wide rack.

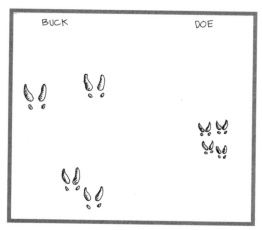

Running Tracks

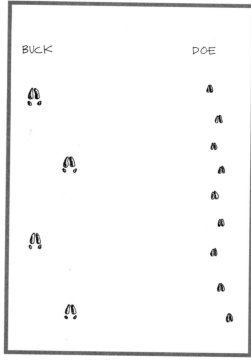

Walking Tracks

HOW LONG IS THE STRIDE?

When a buck walks at a normal pace, two feet between prints is a good buck; anything more than that and you've got a real monster. The length of the stride shows how heavy a buck might be. The longer a buck is, the more he weighs. One of the thickest and heaviest-necked bucks I've taken weighed two hundred pounds even and was seven and a half years old. He was very short and compact. Another buck I shot had a thin neck and I doubted he'd weigh two hundred pounds, but he tipped the scales at 235. Hanging up, he was ten feet long from his back feet to the tip of his horns.

AGING TRACKS

Knowing how to age tracks is very important, but it can be tricky because there are so many variables to consider. You'll have to look at the temperature the previous night, the daytime temperature, the type of snow, when it last snowed, and whether the snow melted or evaporated. Knowing how to age tracks will keep you from sneaking along on an eight-hour-old track or hurrying on a half-hour-old one.

WHEN TO AGE A TRACK

The first time to age a track is when you're deciding whether to follow it. I always pay attention to the weather the night before. I look at the temperature before I go to bed and when I get up. If I hear it snow in the night, I note what time it started.

This way, in the morning I have a better chance of figuring out when a track was made. I'll usually take a big track made any time during the night. Many hunters have the idea that if a track wasn't just made, it's not fresh and therefore not worth taking. I go on the assumption that wherever the buck went during the night I can go during the day. I've never taken the track of a buck in the morning that I did not catch up to during the day, and the track of the biggest buck I've taken was two nights old when I started on it!

AGING TRACKS IN SNOW

The type of snow matters when you're aging a track. A damp snow keeps the track crisp for a long time, and sometimes this can make you think the track is newer than it really is. If there's cold, dry snow on ground that is not frozen, a track will probably have ice in it, but don't worry—it takes only a short time to freeze when it's cold. If snow is falling and you have an idea when it started, you should be able to tell the age of a track fairly accurately. For example, if it's snowing an inch every two hours and there's an inch of snow in the track, it's about two hours old—a good one to take. If you're lucky enough to cut a track that has only a dusting of snow in it during a snowstorm, start looking—that buck is not far away. Once in my training years I picked up a track late in the day. It was snowing, and there was only a little snow in the track. I was moving fast when it dawned on me that there was no longer any snow in the track. I stopped quickly, and when I did the buck jumped from behind a blowdown he was feeding on about thirty yards away. I blew that one— I was looking at the track when I should have been looking around.

If you wake up in the morning to find it snowing hard and blowing, you'll have a difficult time finding a track for two reasons. First, deer often hole up during this kind of weather. Sometimes I've walked all day in these conditions and never found a track to follow. The second reason applies if you're trying to find a track from the road. The wind usually blows down roads, and it doesn't take long for drifts to cover tracks that might have been made. I've tracked bucks in conditions like this when I knew I was less than half an hour behind a buck, but his track across the road was already obliterated.

DRIFTS COVER THE TRACKS

I took Chris out tracking one morning after a fresh snow the night before. The snow had stopped, but it was quite windy. Chris and I dropped another hunter off and were looking for tracks as we went. We turned around and came back on the same road before turning onto another road where we found a nice track. It wasn't more than an hour old, and we had high hopes as we followed it into a spruce thicket where the buck had been looking for does. We hunted slowly, as I was sure he must be in there because the other road we had driven on was only a quarter mile ahead of us, and we hadn't seen tracks crossing it. Then the track went out of the spruces and right up to the road we had driven on and disappeared—it had drifted over. We picked the track back up on the other side of the road and followed it up the mountain. We had now lost over an hour, so we hadn't gained on him at all. When we got up the mountain, we found where he had spent quite a bit of time feeding and looking for does. Then he crossed the border into Canada and we had to stop. We might have caught up to him before he crossed the border if we hadn't missed the track that had been drifted over in the road.

Another thing to consider if you find a track with snow in it is which direction the buck is traveling. If he's walking, it might be difficult to tell. Brush some snow aside and poke your fingers down to the bottom of the track, and you may be able to feel which way the hooves are pointing. You may also see snow pushed ahead of the print as he steps. If you're still not sure, follow the track the way you think it is going, and there will eventually be a place where he jumped to cross a log or stream. His back feet will be farther apart and ahead of his front feet, and you'll be able to tell his direction of travel.

Sometimes when there is

This is what you hope to find when tracking. A buck preoccupied with rubbing and scraping will be easier to spot.

snow on the ground, the weather may turn warm or rain may fall and start melting it. When this happens, aging tracks can be tricky because they'll look older and appear bigger than they really are because they melt from the inside out. Check the dewclaws and stride to make sure it's a buck. If you don't, you may follow a track that looks big only to come to a small bed with a smaller track leaving than the one arriving. You may even find a track so melted out that you can barely distinguish the hoofprints. If you know the melting happened during the night and the track wasn't there the day before, it's still a good track to take.

FOLLOWING A MELTED TRACK

I followed a track like that one morning after it had rained all night. It went up a hardwood ridge that I had been on the day before without seeing any big tracks. I cut a good buck track that was washed out to double its normal size. I thought the buck was quite far ahead of me, so I kicked into high gear and started traveling. I hadn't gone a quarter mile before he busted out of some thick slash thirty yards in front of me. He'd been bedded, and I happened to pick up his track at the end of his night's journey. I shot him a few hours later.

Never discount a track in these conditions—it might be fresher than you think. If you're always looking for an hour-old track, you'll do more looking than tracking. If you get on a track made the night before, one thing is for sure—a buck will be at the end of it.

AGING TRACKS AS YOU MOVE ALONG

Once you've found the track you want, you'll need to keep track of its age as you follow it. This is where knowing the current temperature plays a big role in your tracking. When it's cold, a track that breaks through ice will start to freeze instantly. I check the track by tapping it with the barrel of my rifle to see how thick the ice is. If there's just a skim of ice, I know I'm not far behind. The inside edge of the track also tells you about the age. When a track is made, the inside edges as well as the snow

kicked up in front will be soft. As the track ages, the snow will start to become firm. How fast this happens depends on the temperature. I constantly check tracks by feel. I take my glove off and feel inside the track with my bare fingers. When the temperature stays around freezing, it's very difficult to age tracks, because a track will keep its texture and appearance for hours.

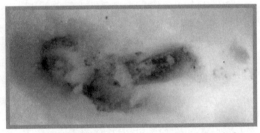

This old buck had a crooked toe on his back foot. it was an easy one to follow when there were other tracks around.

AGING TRACKS BY EXAMINING DROPPINGS

Another way to age a track is to feel droppings. This is often more accurate than feeling the track itself. Feeling droppings is most accurate when it's cold enough to freeze things. I pick up droppings and squeeze them to see how frozen they are. (I know some people probably think I'm nuts, but let's just call it getting back to nature!)

Hunters tell me all sorts of things they've read about how to tell buck droppings from doe droppings. One even told me he had read that buck droppings are the clumpy ones and doe droppings are the individual pellets. Nothing could be further from the truth. What a deer eats controls the consistency of its droppings. In summer and early fall, when they're feeding on green plants, the droppings tend to clump together. When they start eating nuts and browse, the droppings are in pellet form. Pellet size is also not an indication of the size of a buck—that's an old wives' tale. From what I've observed during years of tracking and killing big bucks, I'd say that four out of five bucks have small droppings—when you field dress enough big bucks, it becomes obvious. This tells me that most of the bigger droppings I see are made by does. Another thing I've noticed is that elongated (capsule-shaped) droppings are made by does. If you're skeptical about any of this, the next time you track a good buck, check out the droppings for size.

WHAT TO DO ONCE YOU FIND THE TRACK YOU WANT TO FOLLOW

Once you've found the track you want, be aware that the buck you're following is either bedded or up and moving. If you pick up a track in the morning, he'll probably be bedded when you catch up to him. Hunt the track until you feel he's up and moving around. You'll be able to tell he's up if you find a bed with fresher tracks leaving it or tracks that get fresher as you go. If a buck is moving quickly, I'll move quickly, too. I don't want to waste time if I'm an hour behind him. I'll set a fairly fast pace, but I always look around as I go. I learn something from every buck I track. I may not get him the first time, but if I can learn his habits, I'll have a better chance the next time I encounter his track. I always pay attention to what the buck is doing and where he's going. I note streams I've crossed and ridges I've gone over. I keep a running tally in my head of other buck tracks I cross along the way and which direction they go. This helps me to sort things out if the buck starts circling around searching for does and also makes me aware of other buck tracks I'd rather take. I may find a bigger or fresher track or one heading in a direction I'd rather go, and I'll switch tracks if I think my chances are better with the new one.

IT PAID TO SWITCH TRACKS

We did just that in the story I told of the buck with the cut foot. We had been following a track made during the night since first thing in the morning. It was about ten o'clock when we crossed the track of another good buck. The new track had been made since daylight, so I figured we had a better chance of catching up to him in a hurry. We took the new track and jumped that buck in about fifteen minutes. Another time my son, Gary, was with me, and we were tracking a good buck. We came to a spot that was torn up where our buck had fought with another buck. I was circling around trying to sort out the tracks when I found a bed with a fresh track leaving it. We started following that one and bumped into the buck in a thicket only a hundred yards away. Every situation is different, but sometimes it pays to switch tracks. ◖●

When a buck starts checking on does, he will take some time, and the more time he spends, the faster you'll gain on him. Sometimes a buck will just scent-check for does as he passes by, but as the rut get closer, he'll spend more time following does around. This creates a jumble of tracks that you would swear was made by a whole herd of deer. When I find a spot like this I make a big circle around the

area, looking for my buck's track coming out. I do this for two reasons: first, it saves time, and second, he may still be with the doe. Either way, doing this makes figuring out my next move faster. If you try to follow where a buck and doe fooled around, you'll waste a lot of time and get frustrated. Make the circle and you'll gain time on your buck.

The scene where two bucks had been fighting. It was torn up in an area fifty-by-fifty feet.

HOW DO YOU KNOW IF A BUCK IS BEDDED?

I'm often asked how to tell when and where a buck is bedded. It's a good question, because if you know the answer, you have a much better chance of seeing him and getting a shot. You won't be able to tell all the time, but here are some things to look

A fresh rub on a beech tree. (Note the shavings on the snow.)

for: Since bucks like to bed in secure spots, they usually choose a bluff. If they bed in low ground, they'll probably choose a knoll in green growth.

This doesn't narrow the choices much, so here are some other things to check out: When I'm following a buck and his track turns abruptly uphill, there's a good chance he's bedded, so I start looking at the possibilities. I'll usually leave the track and circle around as high as I can get. On this first circle, I look for his track coming out. If I cross a track coming out, I keep following it and haven't lost any time. If it doesn't come out, I go back to my old track and cut the circle a little smaller. Now I take my time and look everything over, hoping to catch him lying down. I have all the time in the world—a buck is within several hundred yards of me and all I need to do is find him.

CIRCLING WORKS!

Once I picked up a track from a road during a blizzard. I had driven to the end of the road and as I came back out, I cut a buck track that had been made since I went in. I followed it high up onto a hardwood ridge. Up ahead I saw a green bluff, and the buck was headed straight for it. I circled above it, and when I peeked over the edge, I saw him lying down about forty yards below me staring down his back track. That was his last day on the mountain.

If you're hunting with a companion, post one person and the other person should circle the track.

By going high and looking down, you keep the upper hand. A buck always watches his back track and won't expect danger from above. I've also used this method when a buck turns and goes uphill. Sometimes he'll pick a place to bed where he can see the spot where he turned. As soon as he sees you turn onto his track, he'll be gone, but if you circle above him, you may catch him looking around.

The best indication that a buck is going to bed down is seeing him feeding. Most of the time a buck will feed just before lying down, especially if he's been on a long journey. Be careful not to miss the signs—sometimes they just nip a twig here and there. Bucks also frequently rub their antlers before bedding, and sometimes they also paw the ground a little. If you see signs of feeding combined with either of the other two actions, your buck will almost certainly be bedded nearby.

FOLLOWING THE BEDDING SIGNS

Stan and I were working a track through some green bluffs up on a mountain. The buck started to feed as he went down into a hardwood ravine. Then he started rubbing his antlers here and there before heading into some green growth. I knew there was a winter road on the other side of the green growth, and I told Stan to circle around and wait in the road for the buck to cross, as I didn't think we could get a shot in the thicket. I took the track into the thicket thinking I'd spook him out to where Stan was. I was inching along when I heard a little rustle ahead of me. I looked up to see a nice eight-pointer take a jump and stop thirty yards from me. He was looking in my direction and I could see the steam coming from his nostrils. All I could think of was Stan, standing out there in the road and wishing he was with me. The buck finally took off and crossed the road just around the corner from where Stan was standing.

By paying attention to what a buck is doing, you'll be able to take a lot of the guesswork out of knowing when he's bedded. If a buck is bedded and hasn't been spooked, you'll have a good chance of getting a shot at him. When you see that a buck has started to feed, start looking for a place you think he might be bedded and start circling. Move slowly and silently and look over every inch of the woods trying to catch a glimpse of fur or antler.

If you're tracking with a companion, one of you should wait on the track where you have a good opening to shoot, because often when you spook a buck from somewhere other than his track he'll run or sneak out on his back track. I think they do this because it was safe when they came in that way, so they feel safe running out that way. Once they get away from the immediate area, though, they'll

This buck avoided the opening between these saplings. This tells you he has a wide rack. (Courtesy: Susan C. Morse)

leave their track and go where instinct tells them. Leave the hunter who stays on the track at the place where the other hunter starts circling. That way he or she will be close enough for a shot if the buck chooses his back track as an escape route.

BETTER NOW THAN LATER

While driving in on a logging road early one morning during a snow-storm, Stan and I rounded a corner and saw a big buck track going down the road away from us. It looked so fresh I thought the buck should still be standing in it! We followed it down the road to where it went into the woods, and there we could see that the buck had started to run. He must have seen us come around the corner in the truck. I figured that since he was up and moving, our best chance was to try to catch him looking. We followed him as he wandered about a mile down into a swampy thicket. Soon we saw signs of feeding and some rubbed saplings, and I told Stan he'd be bedded close by. We found the best opening we could, and Stan waited. I made a two-hundred-yard circle and was swinging back toward Stan when I spotted a bed in front of me. It had been made by our buck, and he had just left, heading out on his back track right toward Stan. I eased along the track, expecting to hear a shot ring out at any time. When I saw Stan up ahead I was bewildered. Why hadn't he shot? When I reached him, he told me that he had seen the buck but felt the foliage was too thick to chance a shot, and thought we might get a better opportunity later. We tried all day to get another chance but never did. This one-hunter-stays-while-the-other-circles tactic has worked often enough for me that I try it whenever I have another hunter with me.

A typical remote deer camp in the north woods.

Once you've discovered a buck's bedding place, there are two possible outcomes. One, you shoot him, and two, you spook him and he hauls away in twenty-foot bounds. If the latter happens, many hunters give up on the track, thinking the buck is long gone. But having this happen actually makes me happy—I got the buck to move out of an area where I wasn't able to shoot him, and now I may have a better chance. It's human nature to take off in hot pursuit of a buck you've spooked. You think he must be right ahead of you waiting to be shot, but he's not. He's waiting, but he's also watching his back track, and as soon as he sees you, he'll be gone again. Once that happens, he'll probably put some distance between himself and you and will continually look back on his track. As you follow him you'll find places where he stood looking back and then a set of running tracks leaving.

For years I immediately followed spooked bucks, and the most I ever got was a quick running shot at a fleeing animal. It finally dawned on me that if I waited a while before following him, he might forget that I was there. This was another patience lesson I had to learn, but it has paid off tremendously over the years. Now if I spook a buck, I sit down to have a sandwich and wait half an hour. I have to check my watch, as it always seems like an eternity. I've tried waiting fifteen minutes, and that doesn't work. Remember that when you're waiting, so is your buck. He'll wait to see if something is going to follow him, and when nothing comes along he relaxes and goes about his business. Often he'll lie down again. Most of the time a buck does't know what spooked him. He simply saw movement or heard a noise and wants to get away from the immediate area until he can identify what it was.

EAT A SANDWICH FIRST? ARE YOU KIDDING?

One morning I left my remote camp with Brian, my hunter for the week. There was an inch of new snow on top of the three inches we already had, and it was still snowing. We were excited about the day's hunt, since we had already seen three good bucks that week but hadn't had a shot. We knew luck would eventually swing our way. We were hoping to find a fresh track but knew it would be difficult—the snow was making all the tracks look the same. We were still-hunting parallel to each other on the side of a green bluff where I knew several does were hanging around. I saw a deer bust out of the firs in front of me and run down the ridge. I walked down to check the bed and found that it had been made by a pretty decent buck.

I went over and told Brian that I had jumped a buck that would weigh about 180 pounds and it was his call whether we went after him or not. He had really wanted a bruiser, but since it was Thursday already, he chose to go after this buck. I said, "OK," pulled a sandwich out of my pack, and started eating it. Brian said, "What are you doing? We have to go after the buck!" When I told him we were going to wait half an hour, he couldn't believe it. He told me that in Pennsylvania, where he's from, if you wait around, a buck will be on another property where you can't hunt. I told Brian to relax, because the buck wouldn't go far. When the half hour was up, we went after him. When I have another hunter on the track with me, I walk in front so I can read the track, and the other person stays right behind me watching off to both sides. The buck ran only about two hundred yards and then started walking. We walked

Brian with his first big woods buck. An eight-pointer taken after a short quarter mile track-ing job. We gave the buck a half-hour to settle down after jumping him and he bedded again.

about two hundred yards more before cresting a spruce knoll. I scanned the woods up ahead, spotted the buck moving behind a blowdown, and pointed out to Brian where he was. The buck walked behind the blowdown, and as he stopped to look back toward us, only his neck showed. Brian fired and the buck dropped like a sack of potatoes. It was ninety paces to where the eight-pointer lay dead with a hole in his throat patch. Brian said this was a special buck for him, as he had always wanted to hunt in Maine and he had shot the buck with the rifle his father, now passed away, had given him.

Brian shot that deer within five hundred yards of where we jumped him. That was the start of a streak where my hunters and I killed three bucks on three hunting days in a row. The day after Brian shot his buck I shot a 220-pound nine-pointer. The next hunter I had shot a 180 pointer on his first day out. With all three of these bucks I used the tactic of waiting a half hour, and the farthest any of the bucks was shot from where it were spooked was about half a mile. If you try waiting patiently, you'll greatly improve your chances while tracking. :●

Sometimes when you spook a buck, especially in the afternoon, he may decide to stay up and go on a walkabout. He may start making his rounds, checking for does and freshening his scrapes. This is the best time to get a shot, as he'll be easier to spot when he's moving. He'll also be preoccupied when he's scraping or rubbing and is not as likely to spot you. If I've waited half an hour and find that a buck is still wandering, I move right along for a while to catch back up to him. Once I've caught up, I move more slowly and watch what he's doing. For me this is the most exciting time to track. A buck is close to me, I can "watch" his every move by observing the changes in his track, and I never know when I'll peek around the next tree and see him standing there, as if by magic.

The final point to remember about tracking is to always be watching for other deer as you go. Don't become so focused on the track you're following that you fail to see anything else in the woods. Other deer can be decoys and can often give you information if you examine their actions. When you're tracking a buck, remember that he'll be traveling where other bucks travel, and the chances of seeing a different buck are good.

OPPORTUNITY ALMOST MISSED

One day Stan and I were tracking a buck that seemed to be on a mission. We had jumped him late in the morning after working his track for a few hours. Now he was down in a thick spruce tangle where it was hard to see more than thirty yards. We jumped him again, and since it was late in the day we stayed on his track. We had gone only another hundred yards when we came to some tracks wandering around in the thicket and saw signs of feeding. The tracks were the same size as the ones we we'd been following, so at first I thought it was the same buck, but it didn't make sense to me that a buck that had just been jumped would stop to feed so soon. The tracks were fresh, and I was looking around thinking about what to do next when I spotted half of an eight-point rack sticking out from behind a spruce tree twenty yards from us. I could make out the outline of his back and could tell he was standing broadside. Stan was one step to my left and couldn't see him. I thought he was going to get a shot, but instead the buck just evaporated into the spruce, as they often do. If I had been focused just on the running track of the buck we were on, we would have walked right past the other buck and never known he was around. :●

I've taken you through all the steps and tactics I use when tracking bucks. You have to realize, though, that every situation is different and every buck is unique. No one tactic will work all the time, and if it did, I'd hang up my rifle, because it would no longer be a challenge to hunt the bucks of the big woods. I'll wrap up this chapter with a story of a hunt with a client on which we used many of the tactics I discussed in this chapter. See how many you can pick out.

PATIENCE AND PERSISTENCE PAY OFF

It was opening week of deer season and by dinnertime on Sunday night, it had started to snow and it was accumulating fast. All the hunters were a-buzz in anticipation of what the first morning would bring. By breakfast the next morning, over a foot of snow blanketed the ground and the storm was winding down. I told the hunters that finding tracks might be hard, as the deer probably stayed put during the storm. After breakfast we all parted ways, wishing each other luck. I was guiding Sue Morse, as I had the previous five years during this same week. We had decided to hunt some high country where we always seemed to find bucks. As we turned off the highway onto a logging road we noticed that the snow was much deeper here than it was back in town, which is often the case at higher elevations. The snow was up to the truck's bumper, and when we came to a hill we couldn't climb it. I stepped out to size up the situation and went in over my knees. I told Sue we had better go back closer to town to hunt until the snow settled down. I turned the truck around and we headed back. As I drove, I was trying to think of somewhere to go, as I hadn't scouted any places closer to town. I finally decided on a ridge that ran between a swamp and a stream. I pulled the truck down a side road and we jumped out, eager to get going—we'd already lost an hour of our morning.

The plan was to find the track of a good buck and go after him. We started off at a steady pace in a straight line, searching for telltale punch marks in the snow. After walking for an hour without seeing a single track, we concurred that the deer hadn't moved much during the storm. We were continuing along a hardwood ridge when suddenly I caught a flash of brown as a deer jumped off the edge of a bluff. I snorted and we waited a few minutes for a response. When nothing happened we went over to see what size deer I had seen. We found a good-sized bed and a bounding track leaving it. The track coming into the bed was almost completely covered with snow. I figured he must have fed early in the evening and laid up for the night.

I told Sue it looked like a buck worth going after. She agreed and we began our half-hour wait while enjoying the beauty and stillness of the woods. Then we headed out on the track and found that the buck had run only about a hundred yards before starting to walk. Soon we crossed another track heading up the ridge. This track was the same size as the one we were on and was made about the same time the night before. We followed our buck over the ridge and down into a spruce swamp on the other side of it. As we were easing through the spruces I could see a swale opening ahead. As I leaned out to look, I spotted the buck lying under a spruce tree about thirty yards away. He was watching his track intently, and I knew he must have seen me. As I leaned back and pointed for Sue to shoot, he jumped and disappeared into the spruces on the other side of the swale. We sat down and had a sandwich to wait him out a second time.

When we took up his track again, he led us into a maze of tracks where some other deer had recently been. The trees and underbrush were quite thick, so we decided to circle the whole area. As we made our way around, we came to where he had been standing, and we spooked him again. We waited again, and when we took up the track I could see that he had played enough of this game and was going to make time. He was moving fast and circling back toward where we had jumped him. When we got back to the other side of the ridge, where we had started, I realized that the other buck track we had seen in the beginning hadn't gone out of our circle. I told Sue we should go back and get on *that* buck, as he wouldn't already be spooked. We went back to his mostly filled track and followed it up the ridge. When he reached the top, there were green bluffs and ravines everywhere. I decided to circle to narrow down his location. We made a two-hundred-yard circle, scouring every inch of the woods for a bedded buck. When we came back to our own track and discovered that he hadn't come out, we knew things were looking up.

I told Sue to wait in the hardwoods where she could see the buck's back track while I circled again and pushed him out. I went back up his track, and this time I figured there was only one bluff he could be on. I walked to the top of it, and there was his bed with a track leaving it. Just then Sue's rifle boomed, and I was so close I could hear the action work as she pumped another shell into the chamber. The rifle boomed again, and I started down the track to find out what had happened. As I reached Sue, I saw that she was standing over a beautiful buck. She was all smiles, and the first thing she said was that she loved the rifle she had used—I had let her use my rifle to see if she liked it. She told me that the buck had come sneaking down the ridge, and when she put up the gun he spotted her and started running. She swung the bead on him and fired, and he dropped in his tracks. When he tried to get back up, she finished him off.

We took a lot of pictures and I did the dressing chore. Then I rigged up a two-person drag and we headed for the closest road, about half a mile away. I left Sue with her buck and cut cross-country to get the truck. We loaded the buck and were heading for the tagging station by about one o'clock. Sue's buck tipped the scales at just over two hundred pounds, which qualified her for her first entry into the Biggest Bucks in Maine Club.

Sue with her first two-hundred pound buck. I circled the buck and he came out on his backtrack, where Sue was waiting.

Here are the things we did to make our hunt successful. Did you discover all of them?

1. We had the persistence to travel until we found a track.
2. We waited half an hour for the buck to settle down and bed again.
3. We took note of the other track made in the night.
4. We were quiet enough to see the first buck bedded.
5. We waited half an hour again.
6. We circled the thicket when we got into the maze of tracks.
7. As the first buck circled back we noticed that the other track had not gone out.
8. We changed tracks when we thought we had a better chance.
9. We circled where we thought our buck was bedded.
10. We posted Sue on the back track.

If you picked up on most of these points, it's time for you to hit the woods—you're ready to get some practice. I think you'll find that tracking is a very rewarding way to hunt. It's you against the buck on his turf. You match wits with him and you have to be capable of going where he takes you. Once you shoot a big woods buck after tracking him down, you'll be hooked for life. ■

Carrying a light and sturdy deer drag is an absolute necessity for the hunter who tracks and stalks whitetails in big woods. (Courtesy: Ted Rose)

THE EASY WAY OUT

As the saying goes, once your buck is down, the work begins. This saying is very appropriate in big-woods hunting — especially if you're still-hunting or tracking — because it's possible to find yourself with a downed buck miles from where you're camped or where you parked your vehicle. When hunters ask me how we're going to get a buck out if we shoot one way back in the woods, my usual response is that if we shoot a buck, we have the rest of the week to get him out.

Being worried about getting a buck out keeps many hunters from venturing too far back in the woods. In most places where whitetails are hunted you can drive a truck or an ATV to within a short distance of where a buck was shot. I've heard hunters make a big deal out of dragging a buck a quarter mile, but in the big woods that's a dream drag. I can't tell you how many bucks I've dragged out of the big woods, but I've probably tried every imaginable way to do it. Dragging is work, but by trial and error over the years I've figured out the easiest ways to do it.

FIRST THINGS FIRST

Before you start to drag your buck, take care of a few other important details. First, take some good photographs. There's no better time to capture the moment and the beauty of your buck than the moment he's down. His hair will be fluffy and his eyes will still have a shine almost as if he were alive. Take photos before you start field dressing to avoid having them show blood. If you hang a photo of your trophy on the wall, nonhunters will be less likely to be offended by it if the deer is clean and beautiful than if

An ATV can be a big help in getting a buck out.

blood is running out of his mouth and onto the snow. And photos taken in the natural setting where you took your deer will preserve the memory of the hunt better than those taken in the back of a truck or in the wood shed. The camera I carry has a timer so I can take photos if I'm alone or get in a picture with another hunter. Take plenty of photos at different angles and then keep the best.

After the photo session, it's time to field dress your buck, and everyone has a special way of going about it. My way is quick and simple. It may go against conventional wisdom with respect to cooling the meat rapidly, but when you hunt in the north, cooling is usually not an issue. First, don't cut the buck's throat. It's a myth that a deer needs to be bled—one that should have been dispelled long ago—but I still hear hunters talk about the need for it. Besides being unnecessary, cutting the throat will make your taxidermist unhappy because he'll have to sew up the cut and try to blend in the hair you cut off.

Here are my quick and easy steps:

1. Cut around the anus as deep as your knife will reach.
2. Start a hole through the skin and flank muscle just ahead of the penis. Put your index and middle fingers in the hole, pull up on the flank, and then run your knife between your fingers all the way to the sternum (the point where the ribs from both sides come together).
3. Roll out the stomach and intestines, including the anal tube.
4. Cut the penile cord at the anus and pinch off the bladder and remove it.
5. Cut around the diaphragm to release the liver and stomach.
6. Finally, reach above the heart and lungs and cut off the windpipe to release them. If you want to keep the heart and liver to eat, you can save these last two steps until you get back to camp.

I do not cut the skin between the hindquarters or remove the penile cord, because doing this exposes some of the best meat to dirt and air and has no effect on cooling the meat.

In Maine, the magic number for a buck's field-dressed weight is two hundred pounds. A two hundred pound buck qualifies you for entry into the Biggest Bucks in Maine

The easiest way for one man to drag. The antlers and front legs won't catch in the brush.

Club so you can receive the coveted red-and-yellow shoulder patch. For entry into the club, the field-dressed weight is defined as the weight with all internal organs removed including heart, lungs, and liver. There are hunters who spend a lifetime hunting in Maine in hopes of bagging just one of these brutes.

The last thing to do before dragging your buck is to attach the tag. Each state and province has different regulations about tagging. Maine law requires hunters to attach the tag to the buck before moving it anywhere. Make sure you check the law for the area where you are hunting. Some hunters have told me they also mark their bucks so they can identify them if they are stolen. I guess this is a good idea, but I hope I never have to hunt in an area where other hunters would do such a thing.

DRAGGING YOUR BUCK

SOLO DRAGGING

If you're alone and capable of doing the job yourself, grab an antler and go. Don't tie a rope around the antlers to drag the buck with, as all of his weight will be on the ground and his antlers will snag on every twig or log you pass. By grabbing the antler itself, you'll be lifting the head and neck off the ground, and you can weave through the brush and over logs more easily. The terrain and conditions will determine whether you should just sling your gun and go or take your gun ahead first. If the buck is exceptionally heavy or the terrain is flat with no snow, walk ahead fifty yards or so, clearing out sticks and blowdowns as you go, and leave your rifle—and your jacket if you're getting too warm. Then go back and drag the buck to where your rifle is. Continue leap-frogging like this all the way out. It's a slow process, but you may not have another choice.

TWO LONG, LONELY DRAGS

I've had some long drags by myself, and the longest one was on bare ground. It started at nine in the morning, and I got the buck to camp at four-thirty, just as it was getting dark. I shot the buck in the pouring rain high up on a mountain. When I started dragging him, I moved right along on a downhill slope, stopping for a breather when I needed it. When the terrain started to level out, I switched to taking my gun and jacket ahead. At one point I had to go uphill to cross over to another ravine. It took about an hour to travel the two hundred yards, over and around a maze of blowdowns. By three o'clock I had made it to the back of a chopping, but I was still a mile from camp. Fortunately, though, I was only about a quarter mile from the lake I was camped on, so I hurried back to camp and got my boat and my wheeled cart. I wheeled the buck out on a skid trail to the lake and took him the rest of the way by boat. It didn't take long to drift off to sleep *that* night. The buck weighed 215 pounds, and the drag was about a mile, not counting the cart and boat ride.

I had another long, solo drag with a 235-pound buck I had shot high on a mountain. I had started tracking him on the side of the mountain closer to my camp, but I shot him on the other side. I had to decide whether to drag him up a few hundred yards and then back down to where I started or to go down from where I was, knowing I'd hit a road that was somewhere down below. It was an easy choice: I headed downhill. I started the drag at about one o'clock, and this time there *was* snow on the ground, which made for better sliding. It was fairly steep, and I went about a mile in three hours. It was getting late and starting to snow hard, and I decided to leave the buck in the woods so I could get out before dark. I took off my shirt and put it over the buck to keep any coyote that might wander by from having a midnight snack. I made a mental note that I left him in a skid trail with water running in it and that there was a stream about fifty yards away. By now it was snowing so hard I could barely make out the ridge I was paralleling. I came to another skid trail that took me out to a logging road where I hoped to catch a ride with another hunter, since I was about twelve miles from my truck, which was on the other side of the mountain.

As I walked, I kept coming across fresh tire tracks in the snow where one vehicle after another had left the area—probably minutes before. I had walked a couple of miles when a pickup truck full of Canadian hunters came along. I flagged them down, and they gave me a ride to the paved road in the back of their truck. I was half-frozen by the time we got there. They were turning away from where my truck was, so I started walking again. The highway plow truck passed me going the other way, so I knew I could catch a ride with him on his return trip to town. (That's one thing good about living in a small town—you know everyone and they're willing to help people out.) I kept walking to stay warm, as all I had on was a long-underwear top and a jackshirt, and they were wet straight through. I walked about another mile and came to where a tractor trailer had gone off the road. I knew the sheriff on the scene, and he let me sit in his cruiser to get warmed up while I waited for the plow truck. When it arrived the driver pulled the tractor trailer back onto the road and we headed for town. I got home at eight o'clock that night, and needless to say, Deb was pretty relieved.

I called a couple of friends from town to help me get the buck out in the morning. Then I took a hot shower and crawled into bed pretty well worn out. The next morning we had about a foot of new snow as we headed for the mountain to finish the drag. When we got to the logging road, we had to wait for the grader to plow it out. We followed him for four miles to the turn where we knew we'd have to snowmobile in. Tommy and I snowmobiled in to where I had come out the night before and started walking in. It was as if we had entered a winter wonderland. The trees were bent over from the weight of the snow. It had snowed even more on the mountain than in town, and in the raspberry bushes it was up to our crotches. I was beginning to wonder if I could find my buck, as everything in the woods looked the same. I wished that I had taken the time to spot a trail out with my knife the night before (by slicing off a bit of the bark from small trees), but I hadn't wanted to take the time as it was late. At least I had made good mental notes all the way out. We walked in just the way I had come out, following the same ridge. I finally felt like we were close and had started looking for the skid road I had left the buck in when I heard the stream to my left. I came to a skid road, looked up it, and saw the tip of an antler sticking out of the snow about three inches.

We started to drag him in the deep snow, but were not making much progress. Then Tommy, who had hunted that area before and recognized the spot, said to wait a minute. He disappeared into the snow-covered trees, but in a couple of minutes he was back with the news that a wood yard was only a hundred yards away, and we could get the snowmobiles to it. We dragged the buck to the yard and went back to get the snowmobiles. By the time we got back to town, tagged him and got home, it was about three o'clock in the afternoon.

DRAGGING WITH A PARTNER

If there are two of you, dragging becomes a lot easier. By taking a few minutes to rig up a drag stick, two hunters can move along without having to stop as often as one does. First, tuck both of the buck's front feet behind his antlers and lash them there with rope or webbing. Then, break off a dead stick a least two inches in diameter and long enough to give you an eighteen-inch handle on either side of the rack when lashed to it. Lash the stick tight to the beams between two points so it doesn't slip. Now both of you can sling your guns, grab one end of the stick, pick it up to your waist, and push. This

Using a dragging stick will help make the job quicker and easier when two are dragging.

method uses the same concept as driving a wagon with a team of horses or oxen. The weight of the head and neck is off the ground, which helps to avoid ruining the cape. It's amazing how easily a buck will slide along like this, especially in the snow.

DRAGGING IN UNFAMILIAR TERRITORY

If you end up shooting a buck in a place you're not familiar with, check your exit options before you start dragging. Locate your position on a map. Plot it on a GPS if you have one. Look for the closest road, even if it's not the one you came in on. Topographical (topo) maps include most of the old logging roads even if they're no longer in use. They may just look like a path in the woods, but they usually follow the best contour of the land, are a good, flat surface to drag on, and will usually take you to a good road. If you can't find one nearby, pick the best route you can by going downhill if possible. Obviously you will want to take the straightest route you can, so use your compass to keep yourself on track. Avoid going near streams and ponds unless you can get a canoe to them—otherwise you'll be battling the spruce thickets and blowdowns that are common in these areas.

OTHER DRAGGING OPTIONS

Here are some other methods to consider as you plan your way out.
- Use a four-wheeler if they're permitted, as they can follow old logging roads fairly easily.
- If you're near a lake, use a motorboat or canoe to save time and energy. Remember to wear a life jacket if you're on the water, as the water is very

By using a float plane, we saved a day of dragging when this one was shot in an inaccessible area.

A boat is a good way to get to areas with little hunting pressure. Watch the weather on a daily basis, as storms can blow in quickly.

cold and you won't survive long in it if your boat capsizes. I've taken many bucks out by boat over the years. In fact, it would have been impossible to hunt in some places without having a boat available to get the buck out.

• Use a wheeled cart. They are fairly inexpensive (look for them in mail-order catalogs) and easy to take to camp. They're not much good in the woods, but they're great on old logging roads or roads where a bridge is out and you can't get a vehicle past.

• A floatplane is the ultimate buck hauler. One year in my remote camp, Mike shot a buck on the back side of the mountain—the side away from camp. He would have had about a two-mile drag, of which one mile would have been uphill. But he shot the buck about three hundred yards from a pond, and I knew my friend Steve could get his floatplane in to it. We were camped on a lake, so I asked Mike if he wanted to pay for a plane trip out for his buck or make a really bad drag. It didn't take him long to decide on the plane ride. We dragged the buck to the pond, hung him in a tree, and made the journey back to camp. That night I called Steve from a two-way radio and asked him to pick up the buck in the morning and drop it back at camp. I met Steve where the buck was in the morning and he got the job done, saving Mike and me a lot of sweat.

A snowmobile can get you back in on roads not accessible by four-wheel-drive vehicles.

LEAVING A BUCK OVERNIGHT

If you have to leave a buck overnight, consider taking these precautions:

- Leave a shirt over him to discourage coyotes. Coyotes are usually too shy of human scent to go near anything that smells of it.
- Mark your position with a GPS if you have one.
- Mark the area with flagging ribbon or a handkerchief. Flagging ribbon comes on rolls in various colors and can be found at any hardware or sporting-goods store.
- Mark your trail by blazing small trees by skinning the bark with a knife. The exposed white wood will stand out against the gray-and-green background.
- When you get to a road, mark the spot where your path meets the road especially well, as most roads already have flagging ribbons hanging along them from forestry use.

Taking these precautions will help you to avoid losing a once-in-a-lifetime trophy and having him rot in the woods or become food for coyotes and ravens.

The way out is not always easy, but it is the culmination of a successful hunt for the nomadic whitetail. ■

Mike's six-pointer. We were hunting so far back in we had to have him flown out by float plane.

The neck on this buck explains why I call him The Hog. I shot this 260-pound nine-pointer at nineteen paces, before he could get out of his bed.

BUCK TALES
THE HOG BUCK

The first week of deer season 1998 had the best weather conditions of any opening week I can remember. It started to snow the first morning of the season and continued to snow lightly all that week. It made for perfect tracking conditions because every day the old tracks were covered with a dusting of new snow. The temperature stayed just below freezing, preventing a thaw, which can cause the snow to crust. It's the weather every deer tracker dreams of. I was guiding Sue Morse that week as usual, and luck shined on her Tuesday when she shot her first buck, a nice fat four-point. That night at dinner she asked if she could tag along on my hunt the next day. Sue is a forester and wildlife biologist from Vermont who spends most of her time in the woods. She loves tracking animals and does it any chance she gets. I said, "Sure, you're welcome to tag along—just give me some elbow room when I get close to a buck."

We awoke the next morning to perfect conditions. After a big breakfast with the other hunters in camp, we jumped in the Ramcharger and headed north. I always like to scout new areas during the deer season when I'm not guiding, and today I decided to check out a ridge I'd been thinking about but had never hunted. I pulled the truck onto a grass road and parked just as dawn arrived. When I slid out of the cab I almost landed on a nice buck track that couldn't have been more than a couple of hours old. He was headed toward the Canadian border about a mile away, so I told Sue we might have a short chase. I grabbed my belt pack, loaded the -06 and headed out on the track.

The buck wound his way through a fresh chopping, zigzagging to make sure everything was all right in his territory. Usually bucks don't travel long distances the first week of the season, and I hoped he might lie down before he got to Canada. But my luck ran out when I saw the open swath marking the border up ahead. He crossed it, probably hoping to find things more to his liking in Quebec. I told Sue we'd walk the boundary in hopes of picking up a buck heading into Maine. We walked about a mile without finding a track worth taking, so we turned back into the woods, still in search of a toe-dragging buck track. We worked our way down through some fir thickets and pushed out a small buck. We followed him for a while, but I didn't see

The Hog Buck made this rub. I knew he was a good one when I saw the deep grooves cut into the bark of this brown ash. (Note the shavings on the snow.)

the deer sign I was looking for in the area. We left the track and were making our way down a ridge when we came to the tracks of decent buck following a doe and lamb.

They were working their way down the ridge, stopping here and there to feed on ferns and browse. When they got down to the bottom, the buck's trail left the doe's and lamb's and turned up a steep ridge. I could see a shelf at the top of the ridge and thought the buck might be lying on it. I asked Sue to wait where we were and let me go up alone so there would be less chance of being seen or heard. As I eased up to the top I was sure I'd catch the buck lying down just over the top, but when I reached it and peered over, there was no buck to be seen. In front of me was another steep ridge. This time I'd have to circle above to have any chance of catching him lying down, and I figured it would probably take an hour to get above him quietly. He had a decent track, but I hadn't seen a bed yet to get a good idea of his size, so I wasn't willing to take that much time to get a look at him. Instead I eased along on his track, scouring every inch of the ridge. I didn't get far before I heard a snort and saw his tail as he bounded up the ridge from behind a blowdown. I snorted back and waited a few minutes for things to settle down. When nothing happened I slipped up to where he had been bedded. I confirmed my suspicions when I saw the size of his bed: He was probably around two hundred pounds, but could be less, and I didn't want to waste any more time with him, as he wasn't the type of buck I was looking for.

I turned back downhill to get Sue and continue on. I decided to continue down the hardwood ridge we were on and see if we could cut another track. After only two hundred yards we came across another buck track coming down off the ridge. This time the track was that of a monster buck, the kind we call a "square toe,"

This rub was made by the Hog buck. I came across it soon after taking up his track. (Courtesy: Susan C. Morse)

a decision. It was eleven o'clock in the morning, and I would not usually take a track that old at that time of day. But since the buck was heading in the general direction I wanted to go, I decided to stay with him and at least learn where bucks traveled in this piece of woods. We followed him down the ridge to where it flattened out next to a bog. There he stopped to leave his calling card on a ten-inch brown ash signpost. There were shavings of bark on the snow at the base of the tree with a dusting of snow from the night before on top of them.

Sue wanted a picture of the rub, so we spent a couple of minutes taking one. She has gotten me into the habit of taking pictures of deer sign. When you study them carefully, you find out that each sign is unique. Different bucks make scrapes in different ways, and rubs can tell you a lot about a buck. Cuts into the wood of the tree indicate that the buck might have sticker points around his burr or that he has short, stout brow points. A rub three or four feet off the ground, such as the one we were photographing, indicates a tall, long, heavy buck.

With pictures taken, we headed off on the track again as it wound down into a bog thick with spruce and firs. The buck continued through the bog, crossed a stream, and then went into a softwood clear-cut that had grown back to a jungle of firs so thick we couldn't see ten feet in front of us. When we finally got out of that mess we were standing in a winter road that the buck had crossed, but then he had gone into more dense firs on the other side of the road. Beyond that there was another hardwood ridge between us and the main road. I knew the winter road skirted the ridge as it went down through the valley, so I decided to walk that, hoping the buck had crossed it again farther down. As we went down the road, which was so overgrown that it was little more than a moose path, we started seeing doe tracks that had been made the night before. A little farther on we came upon what I had hoped for: The big guy had come back across the road, but this time there was no snow in his track. He had lain down on the ridge the day before and had come back off the ridge during the night.

Now I felt a little luckier—I had a track somewhere between six and twelve hours old. But it was noon already and there were only about four more hours of daylight. We jumped on the track again and saw the buck's tracks mingled with those of does as he checked to see if any were ready to accept his advances. He followed the does back across the road and up the ridge again. Partway down the other side of the ridge we came to a place where he had caught up to the does and chased them around. Then they all headed back up the ridge single file. When they got to the crest, the buck left the does—maybe he figured he was wasting his time with them—and continued down the ridge until he came into a hardwood bowl, where he started meandering around and feeding on ferns and tree mushrooms. Then his track disappeared into the thick slash of an old hardwood chopping. By this time he'd gone only about a mile. I didn't think that was very far for a big buck to travel in one night and thought that he wouldn't be lying down yet, but I went with my instinct and assumed he was. When a buck decides to bed in a place like this, it's difficult to circle, because there are no distinct features and he could be anywhere. I've found that it's better to stay on the track in cases like this, and if I spook him out, I might get a better chance elsewhere.

I asked Sue to stay behind me a little as it was going to be closer and noisier in the chopping. As I eased into the brush, I was pleased to hear dead leaves rustling in the wind, giving me the sound cover I needed for those close quarters. Slipping along with the wind swirling, scouring the brush for any spot of brown I could find, I came to an overgrown skid trail. As I peered down it, I was greeted by the sight of a huge neck and a head topped by a symmetrical rack. The big buck peered back at me from behind a log. He had that look of surprise they get just before they bolt. He hesitated a second too long—I had already settled the bead at the base of his neck and squeezed the trigger. He rolled onto his back before the echo of the shot made it across the valley.

Sue came down and we went to take a look at him. I stepped off nineteen paces to where he lay; he had never moved from his bed. Sue said, "What a hog!" She guessed he'd weigh 245 pounds. I was more conservative and said 225. We took photos and got the drag stick rigged up, not knowing how far we might have to go to get to a road. We were about two miles from the truck and on the other side of the ridge from it. We were in a chopping, and I knew there was an old logging road down over the ridge, so we decided to go out that way. I assumed we'd have about a half-mile drag, as they usually don't skid wood much farther than that.

We gathered our gear and, each grabbing an end of the stick, we made our way off the ridge with buck in tow. Stopping every fifty yards or so for a breather, we made it to the road in about an hour. I consider this a very easy drag when hunting in the big woods. Sue stayed with the buck while I went to get the truck. When I got back we realized we were going to have a problem loading him. The Ramcharger has a four-inch lift and oversize tires, making it a long way up to the hood, but fortunately, another hunter came down the road and we recruited him to help.

When we got to the tagging station, it didn't take long for a crowd to start gathering. After doing the paperwork, the time came to get the buck on the scale. As he was being hoisted, Sue shouted, "Two hundred sixty pounds!" and when the pin settled, she was right on the money. That hog buck now has a cherished spot on my wall to remind me of a hunt for a true nomad. ■

This heavy-racked nine-pointer came to my grunt call when I was tracking him and another big buck that were running together.

DUELING BUCKS

I n the fall of 1989 I was making my transition from lobstering on the coast of Maine to starting a sporting camp in northern Maine. I had developed my lobstering business to the point where I could take my boat and traps out of the water in late October and concentrate on deer hunting all season. That spring we had built our first camp, and I was eager to spend time finding more big-buck hideouts.

We received our first snowfall during the second week of the hunting season. As usual, this first snow was damp, making for quiet tracking. I decided to check out a spot I hadn't hunted for several years—a hardwood ridge at the base of a mountain where bucks frequently traveled. There was a lot of doe activity in the area, and I knew this would draw bucks, as the rut was not far off and they'd start checking for hot does. I couldn't find the track I was looking for that day, but I did find an average track and followed it until I caught up to the buck. He was a nice two-and-a-half-year-old that would weigh about 180 pounds. I let him go, thinking he'd be a nice one for my wife, Deb, to shoot. When I got home I told her about him and we made plans for the next day's hunt.

When we awoke the next morning, we discovered that the weather had warmed during the night and the snow was melting, creating such dense fog that we could see barely fifty yards. I told Deb this would be a good hunting day, so we ate breakfast and headed for the mountain. We arrived at daylight, and the plan was for Deb to sit on a scrape line where it crossed a brook while I tried to pick up a track. It was about half a mile uphill to the scrape line, and we took our time so Deb wouldn't be too sweaty to sit. The plan was for me to find the smaller buck I'd seen yesterday and try to get him to go toward Deb.

With Deb settled in to wait, I quartered (traversed) up the mountain searching for a big, toe-dragging track. I had gone only about a quarter mile when I found what I was looking for. It was a huge track, and it looked even bigger since the snow had melted out down to the ground. I knew it was old—probably at least six hours—but I also knew it wasn't there the day before, so I decided to take it. I had a lot of catching up to do, and I took off at a pretty good pace. When I'm in this catch-up mode I don't waste time looking over every inch of the woods—I just keep moving until I get an indication that the buck may be bedded. Well, this time I got a real surprise. I hadn't gone another quarter mile when the buck jumped up right in front of me at about thirty yards. He had lain right down in his track in a hardwood slash thicket. All I had for a shot was his tail waving, so I held off.

This was a situation trackers hope and pray for—a fresh buck track with quiet conditions and all day to make something happen. As I waited to give the buck time to settle down, I thought of the possible places he might take me and how I could beat him on his own turf. He was heading in the opposite direction from where Deb was sitting, so my hopes of pushing this buck past her were dwindling.

As I started following the track again I couldn't help noticing how deathly still the woods were. The only sound was the faint squeak of wet snow compressing under my boots. The buck ran parallel to the ridge for a while, then turned up a steep bluff and started walking. I decided to stay on the track even though he had headed straight up. I figured I had a good chance of seeing him as it was quiet and the visibility was some-times only forty yards in the fog. With fog like this, I can get closer to a buck without him seeing me. As I made my way to the top of the shelf, I came to a buck bed. At first I thought I had spooked him and was kicking myself for making the wrong move, but when I looked carefully, I could see that this bed had been made by a different buck. There were two fresh tracks leaving and only one fresh one going in. And the buck I was tracking walked through the bed of the other buck.

To this day I still wonder whether the buck I was tracking knew the other buck was bedded there or had just happened upon the other one. In any event, both bucks had now wandered off into the fog together. I was sure the buck I was tracking had forgotten about me now that he had a running mate, but I thought it was strange that two big bucks would run together at during this part of hunting season, as it's more common after the rut. I was getting more excited about this hunt—now I had not one but two big bucks just ahead of me.

As the bucks wound their way through the blowdowns on the shelf of green growth, I took my time, easing along one step at a time, peering into the fog in hopes of seeing one of the bucks before he spotted me. It's a rare day when a hunter has an advantage over a buck, but I felt this was one of those days, and I needed to make everything I could of it. There was no wind to carry my scent, the fog limited the bucks' vision, and if I was quiet and didn't snap any sticks, they would't hear me.

The bucks turned toward where Deb was sitting and made their way into the hardwoods. I followed their tracks downhill, and then I came to something I hadn't seen before. Both bucks had walked two circles, as if one was following the other, about twen-ty feet in diameter. I stood there for a minute trying to figure out what was going on. It finally dawned on me that they must be sparring with each other—perhaps dueling so each could assert his authority. As I continued on the track, I found another set of circles. Now I knew that they were distracted and had forgotten about anything behind them— and the more they stopped to spar, the sooner I'd catch up to them.

I had just left the last sparring place when I heard a buck snort ahead of me. My first thought was that I had spooked them. I checked the wind and knew they couldn't have smelled me. I knew they couldn't hear me, and I figured the snort to be about a hundred yards away, so I knew they couldn't see me. Thinking they must be snorting at each other, I decided to try something. Grunt calls were just starting to get popular, and I had bought one to see if it would work on big-woods bucks. I admit I was a little skeptical about it. I knew these bucks would be able to hear it, so I gave a few grunts. I leaned against a tree to break up my outline just in case a buck would come. I waited a few minutes with no response. I gave a few more grunts, stuck the call back in my pocket, and thought about my next move.

After a few more minutes, I heard a strange clicking noise ahead of me in the fog. I was staring at where the noise was coming from when all of a sudden, out of the fog, all I could see was a huge set of antlers coming through the whips right toward me. The clicking noise was the whips slapping the buck's antlers as he pushed his rack through them. He stopped at forty yards, staring in my direction, but I didn't have my gun up. The sight of that buck standing there is still etched in my memory. The only thing I could think of to do was move slowly and hope the fog would blur his vision of me. Ten feet in front of me was another tree. I leaned over and slowly put my body behind it, out of his line of sight. Once I was hidden, I slowly raised my rifle to my shoulder and leaned out from behind the tree. He was still standing there like a statue. I put the bead where the shoulder meets the neck and fired. He whirled and ran as if he hadn't been hit. I fired twice more as he ran, and then all was quiet.

I walked over to where he had been standing and was surprised to see no blood. I couldn't believe I could have missed a shot like that. I started down the running track and after three bounds there was good blood. Just then I heard a crash and I saw him jump up and run. I pulled up and fired again and he collapsed in his track. He tried to get up again, so I put a finisher into his neck.

I walked over to where he lay and admired the beauty of this majestic animal. I said a little prayer for hunter and beast as I always do to thank the good lord for providing me with a wonderful trophy and meat. Deb had the camera and she was still a ways away and below me, so I decided to just dress him out and head down the mountain with him. I knew she had heard the shots and would figure that's what I'd do. I had about half a mile to drag, but it was one of the easiest ones I've had. It was steeply downhill on wet snow, and at times I let go of him and he slid on his own. It didn't take long to get to the road, and Deb soon found me. Although she never did see anything while on stand, Deb was happy for me. We took some pictures and loaded him for the ride to the tagging station.

We were surprised when he weighed in at two hundred pounds on the nose. I thought by the size of his neck and shoulders he'd weigh more, but he was one of those short-bodied bucks. What he lacked in weight he more than made up for in antlers. He was a wide, heavy-beamed nine-pointer. To this day he's still the best-racked buck I've taken. ■

This is Fat Horns. I shot him after tracking him only a half mile from where I jumped him. He weighed 220 pounds and carried an exceptionally heavy nine-point rack.

FAT HORNS

After years of guiding small groups of hunters, I decided to start taking only one hunter a week. I thought there were hunters who'd like to learn as they hunted with a one-on-one service. I was right and was fully booked the following season. I decided to do the last three weeks in a remote location where the hunters would not see another hunter in the woods all week, and I had found a good location for this type of hunting the year before by tracking a buck into the area. There was plenty of buck sign, and the road in was virtually impassable by truck—we'd have to go in by ATV.

The last week in October one of my guides, Mike Featherstone, and I headed in with supplies and equipment to finish setting up camp. All along the three-mile trail we saw buck rubs. That combined with the smell of the fallen leaves is enough to make any deer hunter dream of the time when he can chase a big-bodied wall-hanger. We got to camp, stowed the equipment and supplies, and started tarping down the tent (we cover the canvas tents with a poly tarp to help better shed the rain and snow). We were securing the last corner with roofing nails when we heard a commotion behind us. We turned to see a monstrous buck standing twenty feet away. He stood there long enough for us to see his heavy-beamed eight-point rack. Then he turned and bounded away. We were probably his first encounter with human beings. We figured he must have heard the hammer tapping and thought it was antlers clacking together. Now my anticipation for the upcoming hunts was sky-high, and I couldn't wait to get back in here with a hunter.

The third week of the season brought fresh snow to start out on. My hunter from the second week had shot a beautiful ten-pointer not far from camp. The third week was going well, and the rut was kicking in. My hunter shot a nice eight-pointer on Thursday after seeing a buck every day. This place was turning out to be more than I had hoped for. With his buck on the pole, my hunter was perfectly happy to hang around camp so I could hunt during the two days left in the week.

At daylight the next morning I was heading up the valley in search of a track made during the night. I crossed the brook in our usual spot and started up a hardwood ridge. I got to a point where the day before the ground had been torn up from two bucks fighting, and there was the track I was looking for. I wondered if he might be one of the bucks that had fought. He was heading into the swamp along

With the right equipment, a stay in a tent can be as comfortable as home.

the brook. As I followed his track into the firs, I saw that he had picked up a doe and was staying with her, a sign that he might not be far away. They crossed the brook and were heading toward camp. They went over a knoll sixty yards from camp, and I wondered if they might have heard us snoring! They continued, then turned back toward the brook and swamp. When they got back to the brook, there were running tracks everywhere from him chasing her. It looked like a herd of deer had been there, but I had seen this situation often enough to know that it was just the two of them. Then they went into the worst fir thicket you can imagine. All the trees were about head-high and hanging with powdery snow.

I checked the brook to see if they had come back out of the firs and crossed it. He had been rubbing alders every twenty feet up and down the brook, so I knew this was one rut-crazed buck. I found no track, so I assumed they must still be in the firs. I hunted slowly and easily, hoping to catch them chasing. I thought they must have covered every square foot of that thicket as I went in and out of it following their tracks. Two hours later—soaked from all the snow down my neck—I knew they couldn't be in there and went back to the brook to look again for tracks. This time I crossed the brook and found where they had run back across it in their own track. I was a little disgusted with myself for not looking around more earlier.

They headed up a steep ridge, and I was thankful to be out of that mess of firs. Just as I crested the top, I heard a snort and saw brown streaking through the whips. I snorted back and everything stopped. The deer were about seventy-five yards above me in some hardwood whips, which gave them an advantage over me. I tried grunting, but still nothing moved. I waited about fifteen minutes and still nothing. I knew they were still standing there, and I wouldn't get a chance at them from where I was. The only thing I could think of to do was to walk toward them grunting and hope they'd hang around long enough for me to get a better look. I bent over, put the grunt in my mouth, and started toward them. I hadn't gone twenty feet when they busted out of there. I guess the old buck figured he had what he wanted and wasn't going to share it with another buck.

I walked to the top of the knoll where they had been standing and could see that it was all open hardwoods beyond. It was ten o'clock, so I sat down to have a sandwich and wait for them to settle down. Once I started again, I discovered they'd run only about a hundred yards and were back down by the swamp. The buck was thrashing the brush with his antlers, so I knew they'd forgotten about anything behind them.

Just then I heard a snort on the other side of the swamp. I knew it was too far away to be them snorting at me. I slipped through the swamp as quietly as I could, as I knew it opened back up to hardwoods on the other side and I might catch them looking. When I got to the hardwoods, their tracks were running up the ridge. He was chasing her again and would be distracted. When they got to a steep knob, the doe went left and the buck went right—up the face of it—where I had to hang onto trees to pull myself up. It leveled off on top, and his track led across it and down the other side into an open hardwood ravine.

I eased ahead, constantly looking down into the bowl. Then I spotted a big hindquarter and back sticking out from behind a tree. I thought it was the buck, and my opinion was confirmed when I saw what I thought was the end of a beam sticking out beyond the other side of the tree. I brought my rifle up and waited to see if the beam would move. When it did, I put the bead on his back and fired. He was over a hundred yards away, a long shot in the woods, so my bead almost covered him from top to bottom. I saw his back end drop a little, and he disappeared from sight. I ran over to the edge of the knoll, but he was nowhere to be seen. I ran down to where he had been standing and looked up the other side of the ravine. Again all I could see was his hindquarter sticking out from behind a tree. I knew it was him and he was hit, so I fired at the hindquarter, and when he spun around broadside I finished him off with a shot in the neck.

I couldn't believe how heavy his horns were. They were dark-colored and palmated—I could barely get my hands around them. He had nine points and looked like he had clubbed one beam while in velvet, keeping him from being a ten-pointer. His coat was dark and his forehead was a chestnut color from rubbing the alders. I knew he'd weigh well over two hundred pounds. He was an old buck and had almost no teeth left. I doubt if he would have made it through another long, Maine winter.

I was about a mile from camp, but I knew that Brian, my hunter, must have heard the shots echoing down the valley. He had told me to fire signal shots if I got a buck and he'd come and help me drag. I fired my two shots and then readied the buck for a photo session. I always carry a camera with a timer for these occasions. By the time I got some photos and field dressed him, Brian still hadn't shown up. Since I was on a steep ridge, I just grabbed a horn and skidded him to the bottom. I knew it was going to be a long, hard drag, so I started back to camp to leave my gun and jacket there. I was just arriving when I bumped into Brian heading out to help me. He said it had taken him a while as he had been stripped naked with his bath water all heated when I fired, but it didn't take him long to bathe and get dressed, as he knew there must be a good buck down. When I told him what I had shot, I think he was more excited than I was.

When we got back to the buck, we took a few more photos and I had to tell Brian the whole story before we could drag. After the story and more congratulations, we hitched him up with a drag stick and headed for camp. Four hours later, after dragging up and down the ridges, we made it to camp just at dark. We were both worn out and knew we'd sleep well with thoughts of our bucks hanging from the game pole. We talked that night about how fortunate we were to have a place like this to hunt. It was like hunting in the old days, living in the woods where we could forget about the hubbub of daily life and not have a care in the world.

We slept in the next morning and then made the journey back to civilization. Once again, at the tagging station a crowd gathered to see two nice big-woods bucks. Brian's weighed 180 pounds and ol' fat horns weighed 220. I had him mounted life-size lying down, where I can see him every day in my living room at the lodge, a tribute to another fallen monarch. ∎

The Sandwich Buck. I grunted in this 195-pound nine-point, after finding his "bedroom."

THE SANDWICH BUCK

D uring opening week one year I was guiding three hunters who wanted to stand-hunt. I had scouted a couple of new areas and had found some good stand locations for them. After spending two days in one of the areas with no luck, I decided to try some new scenery. I was eager to try a new spot where I'd found a lot of sign and some good rub lines. When I had scouted there during the last week of October, I had found quite a few fresh rubs—as many as I usually find in November.

When we arrived at dawn, there was a dusting of fresh snow on the ridges, and it was one of those gray, overcast days, typical of November in the north woods. It took me about an hour to walk all three of the hunters to their stands. With that done, I decided to spend the day scouting farther back into the woods than I'd gone before. The hunters said they didn't mind if I hunted, as they were going to stand-hunt all week, so I grabbed my –06 and started up the ridge. There was just enough snow to whiten the ground, but leaves were still showing. I hadn't gone far when I cut a buck track heading in the direction I was going. It was a medium-sized buck, but I decided to find out were he was going. I like to follow bucks because I know I'll find some good buck sign eventually. He stayed high on the ridge, paralleling the green bluff on top. After about a mile he came into a hardwood bowl and inter-sected another buck track. A little farther on he intersected still another buck track and then another! I couldn't believe what I was seeing. I took some time and circled the whole bowl to make sure it wasn't just the same buck making all the tracks. What I found was that four different bucks had traveled through this bowl. I had found a hub where buck territories overlapped. All of the bucks had come off the ridge from different directions and all were heading down. I didn't know what was down there, but I was going to find out.

I took the biggest track but didn't get far before the snow ran out at the lower elevation. There were too many tracks in the leaves to try to stay on one particular buck, so I decided to still-hunt my way down the ridge. After a while the terrain leveled off, and I came to an old logging road that had grown into nothing more than a brushy path. There were rubs all along it, so I crept along one step at a time. I hadn't gone far when I ran into Doug, one of the men hunting out of my remote

One of the many rubs concentrated in a small area, made by The Sandwich Buck.

camp. He told me that he and my two guides had come in on the ATV to check out a new area. I guess we all think alike! I asked where the other guys were hunting and where he was going to go. He said the others had gone farther in and he was going up on the ridge. I told him I'd hunt along the trail until I found something interesting.

We wished each other luck and parted ways. I continued down the trail, amazed at all the rubs I was seeing. Finally I came to a huge rub on a popple tree. Right beside it was a willow bush that a buck had completely destroyed and a deer trail heading into the brush. I followed that trail, trying to imagine what the buck that had made all this sign might look like.

After thirty yards, the woods opened up a little and were a mixture of firs and hardwoods. I came to another rub and stopped to look it over. Then I saw a scrape and walked over to that. When I got there I saw another rub. As I began looking around I noticed that the deer trail had dispersed, and there were tracks wandering everywhere. No matter where I stood I could see either a rub or a scrape. I knew I had stumbled right into a buck's living room. I sprayed some more buck urine on my pants and jacket to help cover my own scent since I was an intruder in his home. I hunted for about fifty more yards and came to the edge of a swamp. It was eleven o'clock, and I figured this would be a good place to sit down and have a sandwich. There was just too much sign not to spend some time here.

I took my belt pack off and sat back against a big fir tree facing the swamp. I couldn't see more than thirty yards, but it was dead calm and I knew I'd be able to hear anything coming before I saw it. This would also be a good chance to try a little grunting. I gave a few blasts on the grunt tube, got out a sandwich, and started to eat. Halfway through the sandwich I stopped and gave a few more blasts. I took one more bite and heard a twig snap behind me. I stopped chewing to listen and heard another snap.

I knew it was the sound of a deer sneaking along—after spending years in the woods I can easily recognize that sound. From the skip of the red squirrel to the swagger of the moose, each animal in the woods has a distinct sound. Pay attention and learn these sounds, and you'll become more aware of what's going on around you. I threw my sandwich down and got to my feet just in time to see the outline of a buck slipping between two fir trees. He was moving from right to left, and it dawned on me that he was coming along where I had just walked in. His body looked big, but the beam of his antler looked short. I decided to wait and get a better look at him to make sure he was a buck I wanted.

He continued walking behind a screen of fir trees, and as I scanned ahead, I realized he was heading for a swale opening. I brought my rifle up and aimed where I thought he'd enter it. Almost immediately he stuck his head into the opening, looked toward me, and stopped with his body still behind a fir tree. As soon as he turned his head, I knew he was a shooter. His beams were heavy and a little wider than his ears. He was twenty yards from me and staring right at me, so it was time to act. I swung the bead into the fir limbs where his shoulder should be and touched off the shot. As the sound broke the silence of the still morning air, the buck sailed across the swale opening. By the time I had pumped another shell into the chamber, he had disappeared into the firs on the other side of the opening. I was still lined up on him, so I fired again as he plowed his way through the fir thicket. The brush cracked for another thirty yards; then all was silent. I pushed my way through the brush, scanning ahead all the time. As I reached the other side of the thicket, I heard rustling again and saw the buck struggling to get to his feet. Another shot behind his ear ended his struggle.

I took some time to give thanks and admire this beautiful buck. I thought about the chain of events that had brought me to this place in the woods so removed from anything else. I'm quite sure this buck had never seen a human being. He must have thought another buck had entered his territory and was checking to see who it was. I'm sure the buck scent on my wool pants made him even more curious. In any event, his instinct was his downfall. As I examined him carefully, I discovered why his left beam looked short when I first saw him. He had apparently broken his beam flush with his G-3 while in velvet. Then the growth went into the G-3, making it the main beam. The right antler had five points, making him a nine-pointer. I positioned him for a photo session and was trying to rig a stand for my camera when I heard a snap in the swamp just below me. I stopped to listen and could hear *another* buck coming through the brush! He was about fifty yards away and he'd take a couple of steps, stop, and then take a few more.

I wanted to get a look at him, so I sat up against a tree behind my buck and got my grunt call out. I gave a few low grunts and waited to see what would happen. He'd take a step or two, and then it would be quiet for a few minutes. The sound seemed close enough that I thought I'd see him at any time. I was sure now that I was in an area where deer had not had human contact. Here was a buck coming in to me, scuffing around in the leaves, right after I had fired three shots. Just when I expected to see him step out, I heard brush cracking behind me. Was it yet another deer? The answer came when I heard Doug yell my name. My hopes for seeing the other buck were dashed, but a least I'd have some help getting my buck out.

I called for Doug to come over. He looked at the buck as I told him what had happened. He said he knew it was me shooting since the other guys were farther in, and he figured I'd like a hand getting my buck out. I told him he'd figured right— I was about two miles from the truck. Doug said he thought he could get the four-wheeler down the trail, which meant we'd have a drag of only about a hundred yards. That was a blessing considering where we were.

Doug took the pictures, I did the field dressing, and we were ready to go. Since we weren't dragging the buck far, we each grabbed a horn and off we went, and it took no time to get to the trail. Doug headed off to get the four-wheeler while I waited with my buck. When he returned, we loaded the buck onto the back rack, and I sat on the front rack for the journey out. It was a slow ride, but it was sure better than dragging. We got to the Ramcharger and loaded the buck on the hood for the ride to town. I thanked Doug for the help, wished him good luck, and waited for my hunters to return.

When the hunters came out of the woods, they were excited to see that I had shot a buck. I told them to be patient, as there were plenty of deer around, and they should definitely see some. When we got to the tagging station and hoisted him on the scale, he weighed 195 pounds. Not as big as I had hoped, but still a great big-woods buck. (As a side note, one of my hunters shot a nice 185-pound seven-pointer the very next day, making for a really great week.) ∎

This is the buck I call Number 11. I shot him while he was chasing a doe. I stopped following his track to loop around a thicket he and the doe had entered.

NUMBER 11

Before I moved to the north country, I didn't get to spend as much time in the deer woods as I would have liked to. Usually I'd have to wait until stormy weather on the coast made it miserable to haul lobster traps. Fortunately, storms usually mean good hunting weather. My hunting camp at the time was a 1963 eight-by-thirty-two-foot mobile home, which we'd moved to a piece of north-woods property we'd purchased in the spring. Since we'd always stayed in campers before, the mobile home seemed like the Taj Mahal. We had real gas lights, a heater, and a stove instead of Coleman fuel equipment.

The fall weather had been fairly calm—not many storms—and by Thanksgiving week I hadn't been hunting yet. I told Deb I was going to go Thanksgiving weekend whether we had a storm or not. She said she'd go too, but wanted to spend Thanksgiving day with her family. So I headed north Wednesday night and Deb planned to come up Thursday night with my brother.

When I arrived Wednesday night, the temperature was hovering around zero, and there was about a foot of powdery snow on the ground. It was going to be good tracking. I got the stove going, laid out my gear, and packed my lunch. I fell asleep that night thinking about the mountain I was going to hunt in the morning. It was a new place I'd tried the year before and taken a nice ten-pointer the first day there. I still really hadn't had a chance to scout around the whole mountain and was looking forward to doing so the next day.

When I awoke in the morning the temperature was still hanging around the zero mark. The sky was clear, and the trees popped as the frost pushed deeper into them. I had a quick breakfast, fired up the truck, and made my way back into the mountains. I parked the truck at the head of an old logging road and was pleased to see that nobody had hunted there since the snow had fallen about a week ago. The sun hadn't risen yet, but the moon was full, and I decided to walk back in on the logging road by moonlight.

As I began the walk in I didn't see many deer tracks, but the farther I went, the more I saw. After about a mile I noticed that quite a few of the tracks had been made during the night. It was daylight now, so I decided to hunt up the mountain where most of the tracks were leading. I didn't see any tracks made by a toe-dragger, but

Number 11 where he dropped. He had ten points and weighed 213 pounds.

I knew the rut was on and there should be one around. As I made my way up the mountain, I came to a trail that was beaten into the side of the hill. It was obvious that a lot of deer were using it, so I decided to walk it and see what would happen.

As I eased along the trail looking and listening, I saw the brown movement of deer in the trail ahead. I got down on one knee so I wouldn't stand out. As the deer approached, I could see that they were a doe and her two fawns. They came to within twenty yards of me before discovering something out of place. They stared at me for several minutes, then decided to walk around me. Not wanting to spook them, I waited until they were out of sight before continuing down the trail.

I had gone only another hundred yards when I crested a knoll and saw another doe take off from behind a blowdown. She ran out into the hardwoods about a hundred yards and stopped to look back toward me. I was at a good vantage point, so I watched to see what she'd do. She stared in my direction for a while, and then she began looking into the hardwoods below. I thought maybe she could hear something I couldn't, so I focused my attention down below, and it wasn't long before I spotted movement. As it got closer, I could see that it was a good buck. He was coming through a lot of slash and heading straight for the doe. I'd have to wait for him to get to open woods before I'd have a shot. As he approached the opening, the doe raised her tail and bounced away from me up the ridge. The buck saw this and ran after her. I had no chance for a shot, but at least I had a buck in front of me now.

I went right after them, figuring I might catch them chasing. They went up a steep bluff, so I circled above them hoping to have a better vantage point. As I was making my circle, I bumped into another bedded doe and watched her bounce up the mountain. I started to parallel the ridge, hoping to see the buck and doe or their tracks. A little farther along, I saw brown movement ahead of me again—two shapes sneaking through the firs. I got ready, thinking this had to be the pair I was following. To my amazement, out stepped *another* doe and fawn! I couldn't believe so many deer were concentrated on this one ridge.

I waited for them to work their way down the ridge before moving on. I kept working my way across the ridge looking for the buck. There were running tracks of bucks chasing does all through this piece of woods, and one in particular was a monster. With all of this activity, I had a feeling that sooner or later I'd get in on the action.

I came across a huge bed with a walking track leaving it. Once I sized up this buck I forgot all about looking for the one I'd seen earlier. I followed the big boy up the ridge, where he met up with a doe and continued with her toward the top of the mountain. Once they got up into a high valley, a smaller buck started tagging along with them. Judging by the tracks, the big boy was pushing the doe to breed. He'd chase her around a thicket, then they'd walk for a while, and then they'd repeat the process. I thought I might catch them at it here, but no such luck.

They went into another thicket that ran down the back of the mountain. I figured my best chance now would be to get ahead of them and try to cut them off. I got behind a ridgeline to my right and hurried downhill about a quarter mile. Then I slowed down and started to work my way back toward where the deer were headed. I broke out of a fir thicket and stopped to look around. Just then I heard grunting above me and looked up to see the two bucks chasing the doe right at me. They were only thirty yards away and coming fast. As I brought the gun up, they split, with the doe going behind me and the two bucks cutting across in front of me. I swung onto the big one and fired as he crossed in front of me. Before I could chamber another round, he disappeared over a knoll. As quickly as they had appeared, they were gone and all was quiet. As I walked over to where the buck had been when I shot, I doubted whether a bullet could have penetrated the thick brush.

All I could find where the buck had been were a few brown hairs lying on the snow, and I figured he could have pulled those out going through the brush. I started down the track, looking ahead as I went. After a few bounds I found one fleck of blood on the snow. Not a very encouraging sign. I was watching the track ahead of me, and as the woods opened up, I couldn't see the track leading into it. I stopped to look around again, and to my left, behind a big yellow birch tree, lay the buck, dead in his tracks.

He was a beautiful long-bodied buck with a wide ten-point rack. I checked my watch and it was one o'clock. I counted how many deer I'd seen that day and came up with eleven, the most I'd ever seen in one day in the big woods. Since then many days have come close, but none has topped that one. For that reason I'll always remember that buck as Number 11.

At the time I didn't have a camera with a timer on it, so I snapped a picture of him where he lay. I wasn't sure just how far back in the woods I was, but I knew it wasn't going to be an easy drag. I field dressed him and made my way out, trying to think of someone who might help me drag him. As I worked my way down the hill, I came to the logging road I'd walked in on in the morning, and I realized the road was closer to the lake than I had thought. I thought it might be a lot easier to take him out by boat than to drag him. The only problem was that I didn't have a boat.

By the time I made it to the truck, I figured I'd gone about two miles. The boat option was looking better all the time. When I got to town, I found that two of the three people I knew there at the time were still out hunting, and the third was getting ready to eat Thanksgiving dinner. I asked to use his boat, and I got a bonus: He offered to help me get my buck out. It just goes to show you that when a buck is down, someone will usually help get him out. This is an example of the graciousness of most people who live around the big woods.

With boat and help, I headed back in to get my buck. The lake was rough and we took our time, but within twenty minutes we'd landed and started back in on the logging road. The boat cut the drag down to half a mile, and we made short work of it as it was all downhill. We were back down to the lake just as the sun was setting over the mountain. What a beautiful way to end a great day of hunting in the north woods! ■

The buck I call The King. The result of a six-hour tracking job in below-zero temperatures with the wind blowing a fine snow. He had ten points and weighed 220 pounds.

THE KING

The rifle season had ended, and Mike Featherstone, who runs my remote deer camp, and I had made plans to hunt with our muzzle-loaders. I have a Gonic Arms .45 caliber inline. I use a scope because the stock is too high to shoot comfortably with a peep sight. I don't care for the scope, but I deal with it for a week. Mike has a .50 caliber Hawken carbine with a peep sight. We like to take to the woods after the rifle season is over, as we have the woods to ourselves. This season started out cold and snowy. There was about a foot of snow on the ground, and the temperature was hovering just below zero. We decided to start off the week at one of our favorite spots and finish up back in the remote camp, since we hadn't taken it down yet.

We didn't connect with anything on the first day and decided to move to the next mountain for the second day. When we got up at five o'clock, the temperature was five below zero, and the wind was blowing at a pretty good clip. It had snowed about an inch, just enough to freshen things up for good tracking. We bundled up well for the five-mile snowmobile ride to our hunting area.

We made our ride at dawn, and by then it was obvious that with the wind and the overcast conditions, the temperature was going to stay where it was. Mike and I split up, each walking a different logging road in search of big, square-toed track. We carried two-way radios and decided to leave the radios on until we cut our tracks so we'd each know the direction the other was going instead of just checking in every hour like we usually did. My plan was to check a crossing where I often find a buck track this time of the year. When I got there, sure enough, there was a nice track heading toward the mountain, but it was mostly filled in with the new snow, and I figured it had been made early the night before. I decided to go a little farther and look for something fresher.

This turned out to be a good decision—a couple of hundred yards farther down the road, I came across another good buck track. It was heading the same direction as the first, but this track was only a few hours old. I called Mike and told him what I was up to. He said he hadn't found a track worth taking and was going to keep looking. I followed the buck up the ridge to an old logging road where he checked a couple of scrapes. I'd been there before and knew that bucks used this road for a scrape line. I could see that the other buck whose track had crossed the road had been through here as well. A little farther on I came to the track of a third buck who had traveled through checking the scrapes. All three were heading in roughly the same direction. I called Mike again to give him an update. He still had not found anything, so he decided to work his way toward me.

I continued on the same track, as it was the freshest of the three and they were all about the same size. My buck came to a deer trail with several doe tracks in it. He got in the trail and followed the does. As I went along and more tracks entered the run, I realized that these deer were heading for their yarding area. The run continued on mile after mile along the mountain, with my buck's track being the last one in it. There were places in the hardwoods where the run was filled with wind-drifted snow, and I'd have to circle to find the tracks again.

Mike caught up to me, figuring he might as well hunt where all the tracks were leading. I asked him to stay above me while I continued on the track. It finally led into green growth where there was some shelter from the wind. A little farther along were some doe beds and running tracks zigzagging around a thicket, and I immediately knew what was going on: the buck had caught up to the does and found the one that was in estrus.

I slowed down, as these deer might pop out anywhere. I called Mike again to tell him what was going on, and then I began slowly circling the spruce thicket, looking for where they might have exited. I couldn't find an exit track, so I went back into the thicket, hoping to catch them still chasing. That buck was really after the doe. Brush was snapped off everywhere from him knocking her around. By now the tracks were so fresh there wasn't a flake of the fine blowing snow in them. I expected them to come flying out of the brush at any time.

Mike called to tell me he'd picked up a buck's and a doe's tracks coming out of the green growth and headed farther up the mountain. I told him to follow them and I'd catch up if they were the same deer I was tracking. It turned out they were, and I caught up to Mike on the other side of the mountain. The buck and doe broke out into the hardwoods, and another good buck joined them.

All three went back into some spruces. The second buck was a subordinate; he kept circling in and out from the other buck and the doe. Mike and I split up again, with Mike taking the second buck, who stayed above the others. I knew I was getting in close to the first buck, as once again there was no snow in the tracks. I scanned ahead, trying to get a glimpse of them. I worked my way over to a shelf that dropped down toward the hardwoods and stopped to look again. I knew those deer were there somewhere, but I couldn't see them. I slid down off a steep embankment and stopped to look once more. I looked to the right, and when I looked back to the left, I saw the head and neck of a huge buck staring at me from thirty yards.

I swung my gun up and as the cross hairs hit the base of his neck I squeezed the trigger. The muzzle-loader roared, and the buck took off toward the hardwoods. The doe ran out from behind a blowdown and followed him, and I watched them both disappear. I stared in disbelief, thinking I must have missed the buck.

I took my gloves off and opened my belt pack to grab my speed loader. My loading time wasn't too fast as I fumbled with cold hands to get a new bullet started. After struggling with that, I had to pound my ramrod against a tree to fully seat the bullet. Five minutes must have passed before I finally had a new cap on the nipple and was ready to go. I walked down to where the buck had been standing and learned why I hadn't seen him earlier. He had been lying down in some thick firs beside a blow-down. There was no blood or hair where he had stood, and I began to get a sick feeling. I followed his track into the hardwoods for about a hundred yards, and still no blood. I kept thinking over the shot and didn't see how I could have missed.

Fifty yards ahead of me I spotted the doe's face behind another blowdown. I started toward it, knowing the buck had to be there, too. The doe took off to the right, and then the buck busted out of the blowdown to the left, and they both disappeared over the ridge. I ran straight toward where they had been standing, thinking that the buck would try to join back in with the doe. When I got to the edge of the ridge, I could see the doe bouncing down through the hardwoods but could not see the buck. I ran a few more steps to a spot where I could get a better look and saw the buck running straight away from me and below me. I pulled on him again, and as I was about to squeeze off the shot, he stopped at about eighty yards. The cross hairs were already on his back, so I fired, and he dropped in his tracks. I could see from where I was standing that he was a big one.

I called Mike to tell him the good news, and he said he'd be right down. By the time I had walked down to the buck, Mike was coming over the ridge. We admired the size of his body and his heavy-beamed ten-point rack. We agreed that he'd weigh over two hundred pounds, even though it was late in the rut—the third of December. After the photo session, I field dressed him and noticed that one of his lungs had been hit, which was strange given the angle I was shooting from. Mike noticed a bullet hole at the base of his neck and thought that was where the bullet had come out. I said it couldn't be, but that's where I had aimed the first shot. I decided to walk back on the buck's track to see why he had stopped at the blowdown in the hardwoods. When I got to the blowdown I found out why. He had lain down there after my first shot had hit him and taken out that lung. I was relieved that I hadn't missed. I think that when he stopped for the second shot, he was already dead on his feet.

Now we had to get him out. I could see a fairly new skid trail below us, which meant it wouldn't be very far to a road I could get the snowmobile to. We rigged up a drag stick and Mike help me get him to the road, which turned out to be only about a quarter mile away. Sometimes you're lucky—I'd tracked that buck for six hours around the mountain and through all kinds of thickets where it could have taken hours to get him out.

Mike went to pick up his buck track again as I headed for the snowmobile about three miles away. By the time I got the snowmobile and tied the buck on, it was almost dusk. I picked Mike up on the way out and we made our way home.

When we got to the tagging station and hoisted him onto the scale, he pulled the needle to 220 pounds. Since he had probably lost fifty pounds during the rut, I'm sure this buck had been the king of the mountain. ∎

To see mature bucks with antlers like this in the future, hunters have to consistently use good deer management techniques. A place to start is adhering to the idiom "Let Him Go–So He Can Grow!" coined by the Quality Deer Management Association. (Courtesy: Ted Rose)

DOWN THE ROAD

The future of deer hunting depends on us as hunters. We must be willing to take responsibility for educating the nonhunting community about the reasons we hunt. They do not know that hunting is in the best interest of the deer population as a whole. As people leave cities for the better quality of life rural areas offer, they'll come in contact with hunters. Most will know nothing about hunting except for what they've seen on television. By being friendly and courteous sportsmen and women I believe we can win them over to our side.

We also need to get kids involved in hunting, whether they are our own or someone else's. It's important to bring up another generation to carry on the hunting tradition. There's no better way to instill values and confidence in kids than to take them into the woods and teach them about the natural world. If we don't do this, I fear that the deer will perish at the hands of anti-hunters who have no idea how nature works.

I hope and pray for the sake of the nomadic big-woods bucks that the north woods will remain a working forest free from encroaching civilization. These bucks are what they are because they have no boundaries. As I write this, I have seen much of the north woods of Maine change hands several times. Most of the large paper companies have sold their timberlands to other timber companies. I hope these companies will manage the land for wildlife as well as for timber, and I also hope these lands will always be open to hunters who wish to pursue big-woods bucks.

We must work with these landowners to protect deers' wintering areas. Many of these areas were lost during the spruce budworm infestation of the seventies and eighties, when huge areas of softwood forest were clear-cut. As this forest grows back and once again provides the shelter deer need to survive the winter, maybe some of it can be protected to help insure the survival of this great animal. The deer now struggle to hold their own as winter takes its toll in marginal winter habitat, but the numbers of deer in the north woods are nowhere near the carrying capacity of the land.

Another reason deer struggle is because of the coyote. Coyotes are the subject of much controversy in the north woods. Some people feel they are in the natural scheme of things and should be left alone to cull sick and old deer from the herds.

That would be fine in a perfect world, but not in the north woods. Anyone who lives in the north knows that coyotes can and will kill any deer they come across. They follow the deer into their yards and prey there all winter. The coyote is here to stay—that's a fact—but I believe their population needs to be controlled if we expect the north-woods deer herd to ever again be what it once was.

As nature revolves in cycles, the nomadic whitetail will survive as it has for thousands of years. There will be ups and downs, but the whitetail is a survivor that will be around for future generations of deer hunters to pursue.

Take to the woods and enjoy nature's beauty and wonder. As you pursue your big-woods buck, remember that killing a buck is only the result. Enjoy the process—the chase and the journey—and take time to reflect on all of God's great creations. My wish for all of you who take to the woods is to enjoy many safe and happy hunting seasons. ■

Deb, my wife and hunting partner, with a nine-pointer she tracked and grunted in on a solo hunt.